For Wheaton College
from
John Houghton

**The Search
for God**

January 2007

To Sheila,
who has shared the challenge,
the excitement and the toil.

John Houghton

THE
SEARCH
FOR GOD

CAN SCIENCE
HELP?

A LION BOOK

Published by
Lion Publishing plc
Sandy Lane West, Oxford, England
ISBN 0 7459 3305 X
Albatross Books Pty Ltd
PO Box 320, Sutherland, NSW 2232, Australia
ISBN 0 7324 1258 7

First edition 1995
10 9 8 7 6 5 4 3 2 1

A catalogue record for this book is available
from the British Library

Printed and bound in Great Britain
by Cox & Wyman Ltd, Reading

Contents

Preface

In November 1992 I was privileged to give the Oxford Templeton Lectures; this book is based on those lectures. At the outset I would like to pay tribute to Sir John Templeton who founded the lectures and who has himself made thoughtful contributions to the study of the interrelation between science and religion. A book written by Sir John with Robert Herrmann is entitled *The God who would be known*[1]. Its subtitle is 'Revelation of the Divine in Contemporary Science'. The authors describe it as a book 'about pointers to the Infinite that are coming to us not from mystics but instead through the most recent findings of science'. My Templeton lectures emphasized a similar theme, namely that God can be known and that science can help.

It was appropriate that the lectures were given in Oxford. It was in Wadham College, Oxford that in the 1650s there flourished an experimental science club which met every Thursday afternoon for the presentation and discussion of the latest scientific findings[2]. That club later moved to London where it became the Royal Society, the world's oldest scientific academy; the Society still meets on Thursday afternoons. John Wilkins[3], the Warden of Wadham College, was the influence behind these club meetings; they must have been very exciting occasions. Like John Wilkins, many of the members were Christians whose drive for their scientific activity came from their belief in God; they were keen to find out more about God the Creator. Wilkins' last work, *On the principles and duties of natural religion*, illustrates their concern that their science should illuminate their faith. In this book I express the same concern.

I should explain at the outset that I am a working scientist; most of my contributions have been of a fairly practical kind to experimental science. I have no training in or detailed knowledge of philosophy or theology. But it is important to me that my science and my faith should not be held in separate compartments but should support and illuminate each other. Although I am a long way from working out completely the relationship between these two seemingly disparate fields of knowledge, I present some of the perspective I feel I have gained.

I need to make two particular points at the start. First, it is important to realize that the perspective from which faith is viewed is bound to be a somewhat personal one; hence a good deal of what I have to say inevitably has a personal flavour. Secondly, since I am a Christian, much of what I write is from the standpoint of the Christian faith; I shall be referring almost exclusively to God as understood in the Judaeo-Christian tradition—the God presented to us in the Bible.

A further point of explanation I need to make is that I have chosen the word 'faith' to identify what might otherwise be called the religious or the theological view. It may seem a surprising word to use, as in popular parlance it is often associated with credulity rather than with the critical approach of scientific discipline. I have, however, stuck with the word 'faith' and use it deliberately, because the words 'religion' or 'theology' have to do mainly with the intellectual study of religious material. It is necessary, in developing a balanced and realistic view of the interface between science and faith, not only to approach the evidence from an academic viewpoint but also to include the human response to that evidence from as many points of view as possible. Faith includes both the evidence and the response. It is also seen as the driving force for action[4]. This approach to the material of faith is paralleled in our approach to science. The study of science cannot be divorced from its applications and the way it works out in practice.

To make the book more complete I have added to what I presented in the Templeton Lectures some of the material from my paperback *Does God play dice?* which is now no longer in print in its English edition[5]. In that book I developed a number of models and analogies from science to illustrate aspects of faith. Chapters 2, 5, 8 to 11 and 14 are substantially based on chapters in *Does God play dice?*.

Although the book talks about science a great deal, I have tried to present the scientific material with the minimum of technical and jargon words, so that readers without much scientific background can fol-low the arguments. Some more technical material is included in boxes, which can be bypassed without losing the flow.

In brief outline, I proceed as follows. My introductory Chapter 1 emphasizes the importance of putting the scientific and religious views together. Part 1 (Chapters 2 and 3) takes a look at the universe and the place humans have within it. The perspective this gives us on where within the universe God might be found is addressed in Part 2 (Chapters 4, 5, 6 and 7). I then go on to suggest in Part 3 (Chapters 8 and 9) scientific analogies or models to help our thinking about God and the universe. God's nature and how God can be experienced in a personal way is the theme of Part 4 (Chapters 10 and 11). Part 5 (Chapters 12 and 13) explores the theme of God's action in the world, and Part 6 (Chapters 14 and 15) considers the relationship between science and faith, emphasizing the unique perspective that the Christian view gives on integration of the material and the spiritual.

I have discussed the book's subject matter over the years with many friends, colleagues and students; such discussions have helped enormously in the development of my thoughts and ideas. I am especially grateful to those who organized and attended the Templeton Lectures and in particular to David Booth, Paul Fiddes, John Lennox, Ernest Lucas, Arthur Peacocke and David Wilkinson who have read and helpfully commented on my draft chapters. I want to thank the staff at Lion Publishing, especially Sarah Hall, who suggested ways of organizing the book's material and carefully edited the final text, and Rebecca Winter and Nicholas Rous who have been most helpful in preparing the book for publication. Finally I owe a special debt to my wife Sheila whose comments have helped in making the book more understandable and readable, and who has continued her encouragement and support through the long hours of its production.

Footnotes

1   J.M.Templeton and R.L.Herrmann, *The God who would be known*, Harper and Row 1989.

2   LOOK UP

3   S.F. Mason, 'Bishop John Wilkins FRS (1614-1672): Analogies of thought-style in the Protestant Reformation and early modern science', *Notes and Records of the Royal Society of London*, 46, 1992, pp 1–21.

4   In Hebrews 11, notable actions based on faith are listed. The first verse of that chapter, 'Now faith is being sure of what we hope for and certain of what we do not see', emphasizes the solid basis on which faith needs to rest.

5   J.T. Houghton, *Does God play dice?* IVP, 1988.

Introduction

One of the basic human instincts is the search for meaning in the world. People have always looked at their surroundings and wondered why things are as they are. How did the world begin? Are there patterns in nature? Can we predict what will happen from our knowledge of past events?

From the earliest creation stories to the Big Bang scenarios of modern science, the basic urge to seek for truth has remained unchanged. But the search for truth can lead us beyond the natural world to questions of ultimate causes—to the search for God.

1 The Search

Canst thou by searching find out God?
JOB 11:7, AUTHORIZED VERSION

Thinking about God is perhaps the most challenging activity that can occupy our minds (see box), but how can we set out on the search? Can science help in this quest, or is it irrelevant where ultimate truths are concerned? Can faith, which is ultimately concerned with a relationship with God, be sufficient to discover the truth about God without regard to the scientific quest? How different are the methods of science and faith in their search for ultimate truth? Are they opposed or are they related?

Why bring God into it?

In a small pea-sized lump of uranium of the kind which is used to make an atom bomb, about a thousand atoms emit radiation and decay every second. That is not very many compared with all the atoms in the lump which number about a hundred million million million (10^{20}); only half the atoms will decay in a thousand million years. But which atoms will decay in the next second? A good question! Scientists cannot say; in fact, they will tell you quite categorically that there is no way of finding out.

The great physicist Albert Einstein was always unhappy about the principles of chance and uncertainty which lie at the basis of our understanding of atoms and elementary particles and how they behave—so much so that he exclaimed, 'God does not play dice!' But why bring God into it? Does God know which atom is going to decay next?

Need humans today with their scientific background give any thought to God? And what, if anything, has God to do with the universe, or with us? Can he be known? These are questions which this book sets out to explore.

Four attitudes towards faith and science

☐ Four different attitudes can be identified regarding the relationship between these two methods of searching for truth.

The first, perhaps the most common, is that the scientific method provides the only valid way of searching for truth. After all, the stuff of science, things we can see and handle, is much more in view than what appears to be the less tangible religious experience with which faith is concerned. An eminent scientist lecturing some years ago in Oxford expressed just this view[1]. Religion, he suggested, is not now taken seriously, and has by and large been displaced in the search for truth by the scientific method, which is proving so powerful and effective. Although he had no immediate concrete suggestions to offer, it was only therefore a matter of time, he argued, before science comes up with a replacement for religion. Such a view is common among scientists, and perhaps even more common among those unfamiliar with the scientific method.

☐ Another attitude is the opposite of the first: namely, that only faith is valid in the search for truth. Some, for instance, set the trustworthiness of God's self-revelation found in the Bible over against the method of science, which is considered to be a human activity and therefore subject to human error. Science, it is argued, is constantly changing; what scientists think today is different from what they thought fifty or a hundred years ago. Its changing character is set over against the unchanging revelation of God. Therefore, we are told, whether we seek ultimate scientific truth or truth about God, the revelation of God in Scripture is our only source.

☐ A third common attitude is that science and faith are mutually exclusive. It was said (perhaps not completely fairly[2]) of Michael Faraday, the nineteenth-century physicist who was a regular local preacher, that when he left his laboratory he left his science behind, and that

13

when he left the church, having preached, he left his faith behind. The two were kept apart. More recently, in 1972, the National Academy of Science of the USA, concerned about the California State Board of Education's proposal for parallel treatment to be given in school textbooks to the theory of evolution and to belief in special creation, resolved as follows:

Whereas religion and science are therefore separate and mutually exclusive realms of human thought whose presentation in the same context leads to misunderstanding of the scientific theory and religious belief ... we urge that the textbooks of science utilised in the public schools of the nation be limited to the exposition of scientific matters[3].

We may well agree with their conclusion, but the reason they give for it illustrates all too well an attitude which is common for religious believers who are also scientists—that they carry out their research without reference to their faith and they exercise their faith without much relation to their scientific work.

☐ But such an attitude is by no means held by all scientists who are also believers. Albert Einstein once said, 'Science without religion is lame, religion without science is blind,' illustrating a fourth possible attitude towards science and faith. This is that the methods of science and of faith do overlap, and that we have experiences which relate to both, which can be explored by scientific means and also through the exercise of faith. This attitude is assumed in this book, and the exploration of the overlap is its purpose.

Historically, the compatibility of faith and science has posed no difficulty for many scientists, for example those who pioneered the 'modern' attitude to science which began in the West three or four hundred years ago. In fact, it provided much of the driving force for the scientific revolution. Seventeenth-century scientists such as Robert Boyle who is described on his tombstone as the 'father of chemistry' and John Ray who, because he pioneered the classification of both plants and insects, has been described as the 'father of natural history'[4]—to name but two—wrote extensively about how they saw the new science as exploring the works of God and demonstrating the skill of God's design. John Ray's classic work, *The wisdom of God manifested in the works of creation*, first published in 1691, was in its tenth edition by 1735. On what basis did these men link their scientific knowledge with their belief in God? And is this approach still valid today?

The cosmic watchmaker

These early scientists were much impressed on the one hand by the complexity and intricacy of the universe, yet on the other hand by its inherent beauty, elegance and simplicity. They found it to be a highly rational universe, that rationality often being expressed in mathematical form— the most rational means of expression we know. They argued that it had been designed and brought into being by God. Can we still believe the same today: can we argue for its design and for the existence of a Designer?[5]

In the early nineteenth century, William Paley[6] argued that if, on a walk over a heath, you found on the ground a watch with its intricately coordinated parts still functioning, you would infer that somewhere there must have been a watchmaker. *A fortiori* (the argument was even stronger), he maintained, the design we find in the universe demands a Designer. With our enormously expanded knowledge today the intricacy and coordination in the universe are even more impressive to us than they were to Paley. We might feel therefore that it should now be an even more effective argument.

However, as the philosopher David Hume[7] pointed out in a classical work some twenty years before Paley's book was published, objections can be raised to the Paley kind of analogy. One is emphasized by the astrophysicist Stephen Hawking right at the beginning of his book *A brief history of time*[8]. He recounts the story of a lady who interrupted a lecture on the universe saying that she knew better. The world, she declared, is really a flat plate resting on the back of a giant turtle. When asked by the lecturer what the turtle rests on she replied: 'It's turtles all the way down!' That story demonstrates a fundamental difficulty we all face as we try to look for ultimate answers. Each time we reach for what appears to be a more fundamental explanation we have to ask whether, in fact, it is more fundamental and whether it adds anything in terms of explanation to our understanding of the universe. Does it really make more sense to say that there is a Designer behind the universe rather than, for instance, saying that somehow design is built into the universe? I shall be arguing later in this chapter and in the next two chapters that the concept of a Designer removes the need for 'turtles all the way down' and adds insight, understanding and meaning to our view of the universe[9].

There is a further point I want to make about the Paley analogy. The person who found the watch knew of the existence of human beings who designed and built that sort of device. The walker would immediately feel able to relate to the human watchmaker; from the particular design of the watch he would be able to discover something about the watchmaker's capabilities and characteristics. It would therefore make sense to argue that it had been designed and to deduce some knowledge of the designer and maker. Supposing now the same person later on his walk came across a tortoise for the first time. The walker would no doubt be impressed with its remarkable features including

---

Mathematical induction

The method of mathematical induction can be illustrated by the proof that the sum of the first n natural numbers (a natural number is any positive whole number) is given by the formula $\frac{1}{2}(n(n+1))$. It proceeds as follows.

First assume that the formula is true when n has a particular value designated as m; then add m + 1 to the formula. The result obtained is $\frac{1}{2}(m+1)(m+2)$, which shows that if the formula is true when n = m it is also true when n = m + 1. Now take the lowest value of n, namely 1, and it is easily confirmed that the formula is true for that value. It therefore follows that it applies to all values of n.

---

its protective shell and its camouflage. But, because there is not the same sort of familiarity with the designer or maker of tortoises or similar creatures as with a watchmaker, it would not be as easy to argue for its design or to deduce any knowledge of the designer. The part of the argument that relies on direct experience of the watchmaker cannot be extended to the designer of tortoises.

The Paley analogy therefore may not cut much ice for those who feel that God has no relevance. But for those who already feel or believe for reasons other than scientific ones—moral considerations, or the awe and wonder engendered by modern knowledge of the universe—that there is or that there might be a God, the analogy is a powerful one. We may want to ask, therefore, what our scientific knowledge of the universe can tell us about God the Designer.

Not proof but perspective

As we pursue the answer to questions of this kind we are using what scientists call the method of induction (see box). When employed for a mathematical proof, the proof begins by assuming the result we want to prove—for instance, 'let $x - y$'. We then go on to search out the implications of the assumption until arriving at a statement that we believe to be true. Then we write Q.E.D.[10], x must therefore be equal to y.

We are not here looking for mathematical proof, but our method is similar; it proceeds as follows. Let us suppose there is a God who is responsible for creating and upholding the universe. What sort of God are we talking about? Can I learn anything about him[11] from the universe's design? If I

FIG. 1.1 **Illustration of perspective**

17

can, does what I have learnt strengthen my original supposition that there is a Designer? And does this supposition help in my search for meaning?

Paley's argument was seen by many at the time to be a proof of God's existence, though few today would present it as logical proof. But our search is not so much for a logical proof of God's existence as for meaningful perspective on the universe. Perspective is what an artist puts into a picture to convey depth and meaning (Fig. 1.1). We are looking for views of the universe that convey depth and meaning—and that give us insight into the God who made it.

If we want to view a landscape with the greatest possible perspective we need to find an elevated position from which we can take in the grand view with its mountains and valleys, trees and villages, sky and clouds. Other perspectives can be obtained by taking up several such positions so that we can view the scene from different angles and with different lighting. If we are going to achieve a view of God, who by any definition is the greatest Being there is, we must not do so from too limited a standpoint. We need elevated positions from which we can look with a wide perspective. The view from science is one part of that perspective.

In the next two chapters I shall present one part of that scientific view as we take a closer look at the universe. We shall find that, as well as informing us about the design of the universe (with the perspective that might give us about the Designer) our current knowledge also provides some perspective about our place as humans in the universe.

To know just how we fit in is of great interest to us; I want to illustrate this by taking an imaginary journey into space.

Imagine that you are an astronaut in a spaceship exploring a remote part of the solar system. You come across an object on a near collision course to your spaceship and capture it to find out what it is. From its speed and direction of motion you deduce that it cannot have originated in the solar system; it must have travelled in from far away in outer space.

It turns out to be a highly sophisticated space capsule with controls, communications and scientific equipment. Clearly it has been designed with reliability in mind. It includes a lot of redundancy and automation so that if a fault develops it is able to repair itself. Then you and your fellow astronauts realize that there is room on board for creatures just like yourselves; the space inside is just right—in fact it seems to have been designed for humans. Where can it have come from? Who made it?

A message is rapidly beamed to Earth. The newspapers and TV go to town. What a scoop! There must, after all, be life elsewhere in the universe. But what sort of life? It is certainly technically advanced. But is it conscious? Or was the capsule built by some highly advanced computer? And can this life communicate with us? How do we get in touch? How significant is it that the space capsule design apparently had humans in mind?

During the next days and weeks astronauts crawl over the capsule investigating every part of it in great detail. The results are transmitted instantly to the eagerly waiting media and employed in speculation both cautious and extravagant regarding the nature of extra-terrestrial life.

Just as those astronauts would carry out a very thorough investigation of the strange object discovered and would find it to be a spaceship particularly suitable for human beings, scientists this century have been investigating the universe with all the tools at their disposal. It appears to be a carefully designed universe, very suitable for human beings. Has it actually been designed with human beings in mind? Are we intended to be here? And supposing that there is an intelligent Being behind its design, what can we learn about that Being? These are questions I explore in the next two chapters.

Footnotes

1   Sir George Porter (now Lord Porter) in the Romanes Lecture, reported in the *Oxford Times*, 24 November 1978.

2   C.A. Russell in *Cross-currents*, IVP, 1985, includes an analysis of Faraday's attitudes to science and faith.

3   Quoted by A.R. Peacocke, *Creation and the World of Science*, Clarendon Press, 1978, p 2.

4   He is so described in his entry in the *Dictionary of National Biography*.

5   H. Montefiore, in *The Probability of God*, SCM Press, 1985, develops the idea of God as the great Designer.

6   W. Paley, *Natural Theology, or Evidences of the Existence and Attributes of the Deity collected from the Appearances of Nature* (1802). The key parts of the argument are reprinted in J. Hick *The existence of God*, Collier Books, Macmillan, 1964, pp 99–103.

7   David Hume, *Dialogues concerning Natural Religion* (1779). His criticism of the Design argument is reprinted in J. Hick *loc. cit.*, pp 103–114.

8   Bantam Press, 1988.

9   A point argued by the philosopher John Leslie in his book *Universes*, Routledge, London and New York, 1989.

10   *Quod erat demonstrandum*, 'which was to be demonstrated'.

11   Referring to God as 'he' in this book does not imply that I associate God exclusively with masculine qualities.

PART 1

Our Place in the Universe

Beginning from the hypothesis of God as Designer of the universe, what are its implications? The next two chapters will study current theories of the origin and development of the universe and of our own place in it, in the hope of shedding some light on God's nature and what that means for us.

2 The Big Bang and All That

Order is heaven's first law.
ALEXANDER POPE

Scientists this century have been investigating the universe with all the tools at their disposal. In this chapter I present some of their discoveries.

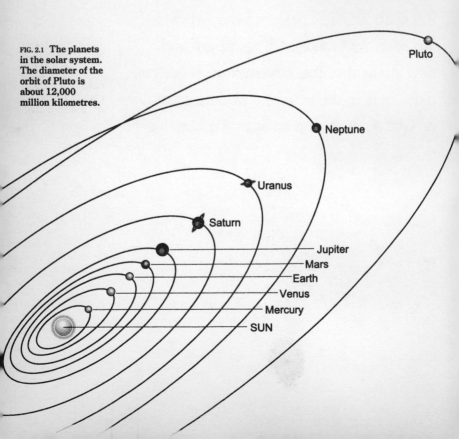

FIG. 2.1 **The planets in the solar system. The diameter of the orbit of Pluto is about 12,000 million kilometres.**

Pluto

Neptune

Uranus

Saturn

Jupiter

Mars

Earth

Venus

Mercury

SUN

In the time taken to write this sentence, the furthest galaxies which can be seen with our telescopes have moved away from us another million miles. The universe is expanding; stars and galaxies are rushing apart. I say 'rushing apart' because they are moving at speeds which, by our everyday standards, are very high indeed. Yet, because of the vastness of space, these movements appear as very slow. The positions of the stars and constellations in the night sky are not very different for us from what they were for the people who looked out on them at the beginning of recorded human history.

Just how vast is the universe as we now know it? Let us begin with our solar system, consisting of our sun with its nine planets orbiting around it (Fig 2.1). The sun, some one and a half million kilometres in diameter—about a million

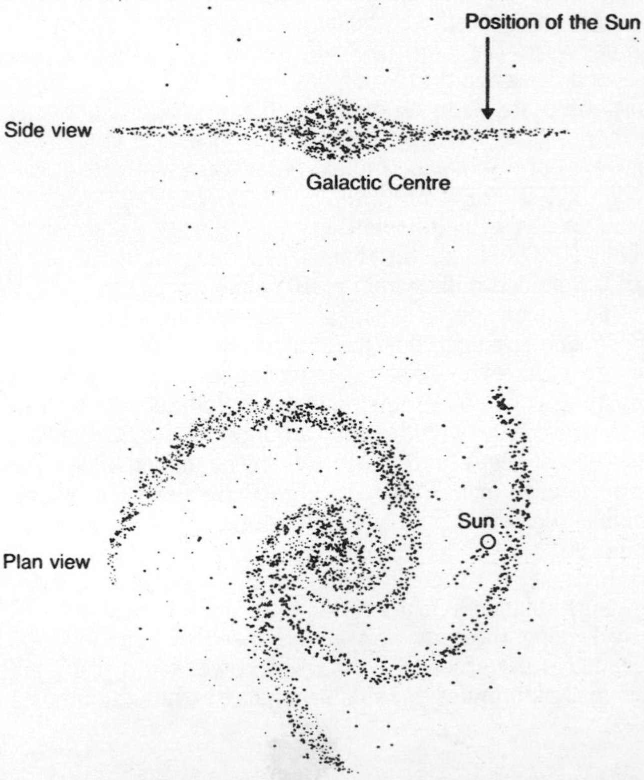

FIG. 2.2 Our galaxy seen perpendicular to the disc and seen edge on[1]. Our sun is 30,000 light-years $(3 \times 10^{17} \text{km})$ from the galaxy's centre.

Earths would fit inside it—is about 150 million kilometres away from planet Earth and about 6,000 million kilometres from Pluto, the furthest away of the nine planets.

Our sun is a modest member of a collection of stars known as a galaxy (Fig 2.2), of an overall shape rather like a flat disc stretching across the sky in what we see as the Milky Way. The sun resides in one of the galaxy's spiral arms about halfway from the centre to the edge. The whole galaxy, which is slowly rotating as it moves through space, is about a million million million (10^{18}) kilometres across. The size of the galaxy is breathtaking enough; but even more breathtaking is the number of stars it contains: about 100 thousand million (10^{11}), the nearest of which is some 40 million million (4×10^{13}) kilometres away.

That is just our galaxy! Close by our galaxy are two smaller galaxies, the Magellanic Clouds, which appear as smudges in the night sky of the Southern-Hemisphere. Beyond them are thirty galaxies within distances of about forty times the diameter of our galaxy, which form our local group of galaxies. Other groups and clusters of galaxies—upwards of a thousand million galaxies in all—are spread more or less uniformly through the universe, the furthest galaxies accessible to our telescopes being at a distance of about 100,000 times the diameter of our galaxy or about 100,000 million million million (10^{23}) kilometres.

To try to appreciate these distances, imagine a scale model of a size such that the sun and all the planets would fit into a typical house. The sun would be about the size of a pea; the Earth and the other planets would be specks of dust. The nearest star would still be a hundred kilometres away, the farthest edge of the galaxy well over a million kilometres and the edge of the universe a good fraction of a million million kilometres from us—still completely mind-boggling numbers.

Because of these enormous numbers, astronomers measure distances in terms of the time it would take to travel along them moving at the speed of light (300,000 kilometres per second). At this speed we would reach the sun in eight minutes; the sun is therefore eight light-minutes away. We would reach the nearest star in about four years (it is four light-years away), the edge of our galaxy in about 100,000 years and the edge of the universe in about 10,000 million (10^{10}) years.

Measuring distances in light-years is a reminder that the light by which we see stars and galaxies has taken a long time to reach us. We do not therefore see these objects as they are now but as they were some time ago, when the light left them. We see the sun as it was eight minutes ago; the nearest star as it was four years ago. When a dramatic supernova explosion was observed on 23 February 1987, an event was being observed which had occurred some 155,000 years earlier. A giant galaxy near to the edge of the universe, viewed through one of our largest telescopes, is observed as it was about ten thousand million years ago.

Since no information can travel faster than the speed of light, there is no means by which we can discover what has happened to those far-off galaxies since then. However, viewing the more distant parts of the universe as they were a long time ago provides information about what the universe was like much earlier in its history. In fact, by looking at objects at different distances from us and therefore at different periods back in time, we can learn something of how the universe has evolved. Some of the evidence will be presented later in the chapter, but the conclusion that astronomers and cosmologists have reached as they have put together the historical jigsaw is that some fifteen thousand million years ago,[2] the mass and energy in the universe was all concentrated in a central mass at extremely high density, pressure and temperature, and that the universe as we know it began to expand from that time, which has become known as the Big Bang.

Scientists from many parts of physics, from astronomy and from cosmology have combined to piece together events since the Big Bang[2] (Fig. 2.3). Our present knowledge does not enable us to go right back to the start, to time equal to zero. But we can come close to it. Let us take a few snapshots of the expansion.

By about a hundredth of a second after the Big Bang, the universe had already expanded a great deal. Matter and radiation at enormously high temperature (about a hundred thousand million degrees Celsius) and enormously high density made up the universe. A cricket ball made of this material would weigh a million tons. The radiation was mostly electromagnetic radiation (which includes X-rays, ultraviolet light, visible light, infrared radiation and radio waves). Radiation at these enormously high temperatures readily interchanges with matter, in the form of a few elementary particles such as electrons. In the extreme conditions of this 'particle-and-energy soup', as it is colloquially called, no atoms or molecules could survive. Even the nuclei of simple atoms would be broken down into the smaller particles of which they are composed.

We have to wait for three or four minutes in the rapidly expanding universe before the temperature is down to a mere thousand million degrees (still very much hotter than the centre of a hydrogen bomb) and the density perhaps ten times that of water. Under these conditions, plenty of hydrogen nuclei, which contain only one proton and no neutrons, are present. Subatomic particles such as protons and neutrons can also stick together to form, for instance, nuclei of helium, each with two protons and two neutrons— a particularly stable combination.

FIG. 2.3 The evolution of the universe.

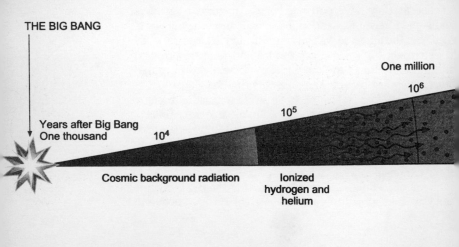

THE BIG BANG

One million

10^6

Years after Big Bang
One thousand 10^4

10^5

Cosmic background radiation

Ionized hydrogen and helium

26

The expansion continues. Hydrogen and helium nuclei are present in abundance; so is radiation. It takes about a million years for the universe to cool enough for electrons to attach themselves to the nuclei to form atoms. By this time the universe is largely empty space filled with sparse, comparatively chilly, clouds of hydrogen and helium gas with only a few atoms per cubic centimetre and a temperature of a few thousand degrees.

Imagine a region within these swirling clouds of higher density than the rest. The force of gravity will attract more matter into this more dense region. Higher-density blobs within this region where matter is more concentrated will contract further. Over a period of millions of years, these high-density blobs will become stars and groups of stars will become galaxies.

As the hydrogen and helium gas concentrate into stars and the pressure increases, so does the temperature (for the same reason that the air in a bicycle pump becomes warm when the air in it is compressed). Temperatures of millions of degrees Celsius are reached. Within these stellar furnaces, nuclear synthesis takes place. As hydrogen nuclei fuse together to become helium, a lot of energy is released; that is the source from which our sun acquires its energy. As the

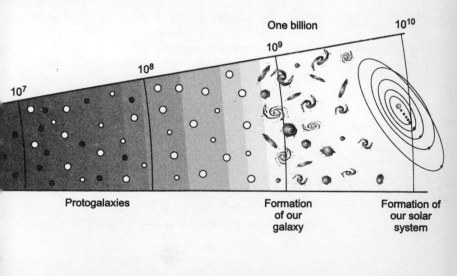

10^7 10^8 One billion 10^9 10^{10}

Protogalaxies   Formation of our galaxy   Formation of our solar system hydrogen is used up, the star contracts and the temperature rises further. In these more extreme conditions, helium nuclei fuse to form carbon and oxygen. Successively, more complex nuclear reactions occur, forming heavier elements all the way up the periodic table to iron. The ambition of the alchemist to change elements from one form to another is in fact a continual cosmic process, occurring on an enormous scale within a million million stellar furnaces.

Even more extreme conditions are generated as some stars towards the end of their lives blow themselves apart in events known as supernovae. We have already referred to such an explosion in the Large Magellanic Cloud which was observed from Earth on 23 February 1987. It is in these gigantic explosions that heavy elements such as platinum, gold, uranium and a host of others are formed[4].

This exploded material contains in various abundances all ninety-two naturally occurring elements of the periodic table. In its turn it mixes with hydrogen and helium gas from the interstellar medium, to go again through the stellar evolutionary process. Second-generation stars are born, containing debris from the disintegration of the first generation. We believe our sun to be such a second-generation star. Around our sun, planets have formed, probably as gas-and-dust clouds surrounding the young sun gradually fused together into a number of dense objects. Planet Earth was born some 4.5 thousand million years ago with its rich chemical composition and conditions suitable for the development of life.

Such is the story of the universe as currently understood, very briefly told. It is a truly fantastic story. But how is it possible that, Earthbound as we are, we can find out such detail about the universe around us?

What scientists have done is to analyze in great detail the radiation that comes to us over the whole range of what we call the electromagnetic spectrum. We are familiar enough with the part of the spectrum to which our eyes are sensitive. We see it in the rainbow, violet or blue light at short wavelengths and red light at the longer wavelength end. But not only does visible light reach us from the vast variety of stars and other objects in the universe. Beyond the

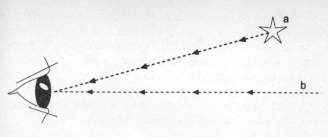

FIG. 2.4 **Olbers' paradox: the sky between the stars is dark at night. Some lines of sight do not end up on stars or other bright objects.**

blue end of the spectrum there are the ultraviolet and X-rays; beyond the red are the infrared and radio waves. All have their own particular story to tell. Since not all wavelengths can penetrate the Earth's atmosphere, some have to be investigated by taking telescopes up into space. This wealth of radiation is full of clues about the processes going on in the universe, not only now but at all stages of the universe's history. Putting information together from all these sources is like a gigantic detective operation. Let me mention in historical order four of the main building blocks which make up the evidence on which the story is based[5].

☐ First, there is the rather obvious fact that the sky at night is dark between the stars. This may seem too simple an observation to have much importance; that it is significant was first pointed out by a German physician, Olbers, in 1826. It means that there can be only a finite number of stars accessible to observation. In a universe with an infinite population of stars, any direction of view would end up on a star, so that the sky would appear bright all over (Fig. 2.4). In a finite but static universe, stars would attract each other by gravity and would move towards each other first slowly, then more rapidly; such a universe would be unstable and contract. The other possibility, surprisingly not appreciated by Olbers or others in the last century, is of a universe of finite age with galaxies and stars moving apart from each other—that is, the expanding universe I have described[6].

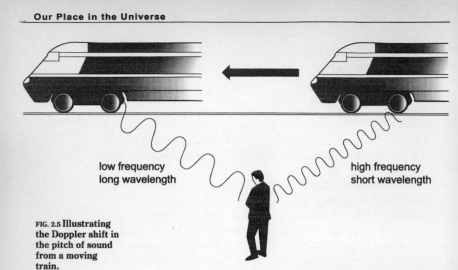

low frequency
long wavelength

high frequency
short wavelength

FIG. 2.5 **Illustrating the Doppler shift in the pitch of sound from a moving train.**

☐ Other evidence for expansion came with the classic work of Hubble in the 1920s, from observations of what is known as the red shift. Light from faint and therefore distant stars or galaxies is much redder in colour than that from comparatively nearby stars. This shift to the longer wavelengths at the red end of the spectrum occurs because these stars are moving rapidly away from us— in exactly the same way as the pitch of sound lowers (and the wavelength of sound increases) as an ambulance or police siren passes by us and recedes— the Doppler shift (Fig. 2.5). The more distant the galaxy is from us, the more rapidly it is moving away. The most distant galaxies we can observe are moving away from us at an incredible 200,000 kilometres per second: over half the speed of light.

☐ A third piece of evidence, crucial in the establishment of the Big Bang theory, came in 1965 when radio engineers at the Bell Laboratories in the USA demonstrated the presence of background radio emission from outer space. This background radiation which pervades all space is just what is left of the radiation present in such large

quantities at the universe's beginning—a faint echo of
the Big Bang. As the universe has expanded, so has the
radiation, cooling from the billion degrees or so a minute
after the Big Bang to the $3K^7$ which is now the
temperature of intergalactic space.

☐ The fourth piece of evidence comes from the relative
abundance of hydrogen and helium in the universe, a
quantity which astronomers can easily measure. As I
have mentioned, three minutes after the Big Bang,
conditions of density and temperature were right for
helium nuclei to form, the ratio of helium to hydrogen
being determined by the precise conditions of
temperature and density which prevailed. From the
average density of the present universe with its 3K
background radiation, the conditions which prevailed
during the first few minutes of the universe's history
can be estimated. Three minutes after the Big Bang the
conditions were such that about one quarter of the nuclei
formed would be helium, the rest being hydrogen—just
the ratio which is now observed.

What about the process of nuclear synthesis taking place in
stars and supernova explosions? How can we be sure that
our understanding here is correct?

Although the conditions prevailing in the interiors of
stars cannot be reproduced at all easily in the laboratory,
over the past twenty years nuclear physicists have
employed many different types of nuclear accelerator in
which collisions at high energy between different particles
and nuclei can be observed. From the mass of data which
has thereby been obtained, inferences have been drawn
about the efficiency of different nuclear transformations
(see for instance Fig. 3.2). The relative abundances of
different elements produced in cosmic processes estimated
from this data fit in well with the observational evidence of
the abundance of the elements in the universe.

We see that some large pieces of the jigsaw of evidence
fit together rather well. Astronomers still argue extensively
about many of the smaller pieces. They are also puzzled by

the remarkable coincidences which seem to appear in the story. These I shall be addressing in the next chapter.

Footnotes

1   Adapted from David Wilkinson, *God, the Big Bang and Stephen Hawking*, Monarch, 1993, p 26.

2   Some recent observations from the Hubble Space Telescope have called into question this figure of about 15 billion years and are suggesting an age as low as 8 billion years. However, there will be a great deal of debate concerning all the evidence before the figure of about 15 billion years is revised.

3   See for instance S. Weinberg, *The First Three Minutes*, Andre Deutsch, 1977.

4   See article, 'The Earth's elements', R.P. Kirschner, *Sci. Amer.* October 1994, pp 37–43.

5   A popular account of the history of modern cosmology can be found in T. Ferris, *The Red Limit*, Corgi, 1979.

6   An article by John Maddox, 'Olbers' paradox has more to teach', *Nature*, **349**, 1991, p 363, explains some of the complications associated with the interpretation of Olbers' paradox.

7   On the absolute or Kelvin scale of temperature, 0° Celsius is 273K (K stands for degrees Kelvin) and absolute zero—0K—is minus 273°C. At absolute zero all matter is in its state of lowest energy; temperatures below absolute zero cannot exist.

3 Made with Humans in Mind?

What is man that you are mindful of him?
PSALM 8:4

Very briefly in the last chapter I outlined the story of the universe from the moment of the Big Bang to the formation of planet Earth. The physics that applies in the farthest galaxies, thousands of millions of years removed in time, is also the physics which describes the basic building blocks of matter, investigated in big particle accelerators or in careful laboratory experiments—and the same physics which applies in the intricate molecular forms of living matter. The humans formed of this complex living machinery can look out on distant stars and galaxies. Was the universe made with humans in mind?

Fine-tuning

As we saw in the last chapter, the ninety-two elements from which we are made have been formed in stellar nuclear furnaces and exploding supernovae and then recycled, as stars die and are reborn. For human beings to exist, it can be argued that the whole universe is needed. It needs to be old enough (and therefore large enough) for at least one generation of stars to have evolved and died, to produce the heavy elements, and then for there to be enough time for a second-generation star like our sun to form with its system of planets. Further, there have to be the right conditions on Earth for life to develop, survive and flourish. But that is not all. Our current understanding is that for the universe to develop in the right way, incredibly precise fine-tuning has been required in its basic structure and in the conditions at the time of the Big Bang. Let us look at some examples.

☐ First of all, the universe is extremely 'flat', the word 'flat' describing the extremely small curvature of Einstein's space-time in the universe. What does all that mean?

Ever since the Big Bang some fifteen billion years ago the universe has been expanding. Because of the force of gravity, matter in the universe—stars, galaxies and so-called dark matter—attracts other matter and acts so as to slow down the expansion.

Will the universe continue to expand for ever? That depends on the average density of matter which can slow down the expansion. Calculation shows that if the density of the universe now is less on average than about three atoms per cubic metre the universe will carry on expanding for ever; if it is greater than this amount the expansion will eventually come to an end and the universe will recollapse. If the average density is just right, between these two possibilities is a 'flat' universe; the expansion goes on, eventually just coming to a halt.

This flatness is of importance for the evolution of the universe as we know it. If the expansion had been too rapid, there would not have been time, before matter became too thinly spread, for the development of galaxies and stars to take place. If it had been too slow it would have come to a halt and started to recollapse already—again, not leaving enough time for galaxies, stars and life to evolve. We are not sure how precisely 'flat' the universe is. But it is very close to being flat. For this near flatness to be realized, conditions near the beginning of the Big Bang itself must have been set extremely precisely. If we go back to the earliest time[1] at which our theories of physics are thought to have any validity, the density of the universe at that time must have been set with an accuracy of one part in 10^{60}. As John Gribbin and Martin Rees[2] point out, changing that density parameter at that time either way by a fraction given by a decimal point followed by 60 zeros and a 1 would have made the universe unsuitable for life as we know it. It is the same sort of accuracy which would be achieved by hitting a target one millimetre across at the distance of the furthest objects in the universe. Fine-tuning indeed!

☐ A second important initial parameter is the smoothness of the early universe. If matter had been initially distributed too uniformly, there would not have been regions of higher density which could have formed the early galaxies. If, on the other hand, matter had been distributed in too lumpy a fashion the universe would have been dominated by gigantic black holes. The universe had to be rough enough, but not too rough, for life to have emerged—variations in average density of about 1 part in 100,000 were required[3].

The smoothness of the early universe to about this extent has been demonstrated by observations of the background microwave radiation from a satellite launched in 1992 by the National Aeronautics and Space Administration of the United States—the Cosmic Background Explorer (COBE). A very sensitive radiometer on board the spacecraft measured 'ripples' (with proportional temperature variations of between 1 and 2 parts in 100,000 in the microwave background[4]) which had been travelling to reach the space instrument since early in the formation of the universe.

These first two examples of fine-tuning concern the conditions required very near the time of the Big Bang itself to allow the subsequent formation of galaxies and generations of stars.

☐ A further illustration of the absolutely unique conditions in the Big Bang is provided by a consideration of the 'entropy' or disorderliness of the universe. One of the universal laws of physics is the second law of thermo-dynamics, which states that entropy always increases with time. Put crudely it formalizes our common ex-perience that things tend to move to situations of greater and greater disorder; the cup falls off the table and breaks, but it cannot so easily be put together again;

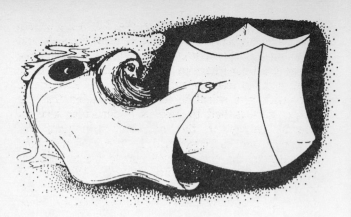

FIG. 3.1 **In order to produce a universe resembling the one in which we live, the Creator would have to aim for an absurdly tiny volume of the 'phase space' of possible universes. The pin and the spot aimed for are not drawn to scale! (after Penrose[5]).**

the scrambled egg cannot be unscrambled; hot and cold objects when put together tend to reach a uniform temperature and do not spontaneously become hot and cold objects again.

Entropy has been increasing ever since the Big Bang, which means that the early moments of the universe must have been a time of extremely low entropy when the state of the universe was extremely highly ordered. The Oxford mathematics professor Roger Penrose has considered the entropy of the early universe and just how special it had to be. He estimates that of all the possible early universes, it had to be special to the tune of one part in $10^{(10^{123})}$[6] (Fig. 3.1). This is a ridiculously large number. It cannot be written down in our ordinary notation; it has many more zeros than the number of particles in the universe!

Further fine-tuning requirements concern the generation of the chemical elements inside stars. Let me give two examples.

☐ During the 1950s, in the early days of the study of the synthesis of atomic nuclei inside stars, one of the outstanding problems concerned the manufacture of carbon. A carbon nucleus of mass 12 on the atomic scale can only be formed if three helium nuclei each of mass 4 collide and stick together (Fig. 3.2) or if a helium nucleus and a beryllium nucleus of mass 8 collide and stick together. For nuclei to stick together easily the energy conditions have to be just right; there has to be what is called resonance (see box). It was Fred Hoyle who, with rare scientific insight, suggested that the carbon nucleus had to possess a particular level of internal energy if the necessary conditions for resonance were to be satisfied. He predicted just what the value of the energy level should be. Subsequent measurements confirmed its existence. Without the presence of this resonant energy level, enough carbon for the generation of life as we know it would not be formed[7].

☐ The story about carbon production does not end there, because it is also necessary that the carbon is not all used up itself in the formation of heavier nuclei, in particular of oxygen. A nucleus of carbon-12 and one of helium-4

Resonance: a condition for life

Just as, to use a lift to reach one particular floor of a building, the lift needs to rise or fall to exactly the right level, so the energy levels of two nuclei coming together need to match in order for a bond to be made between them. This condition is called resonance.

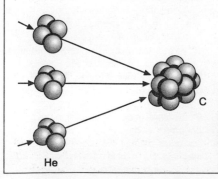

FIG. 3.2 **When three helium nuclei come together to make up the nucleus of a carbon atom, a critical resonance in the structure of the carbon nucleus assists this transformation, ensuring that carbon—of vital importance to the formation of life—is relatively abundant in the universe.**

can combine to form oxygen-16. A potential resonance exists which could make this process an efficient one, but the relevant energy level in the oxygen nucleus turns out to be 1 per cent too high, so only relatively small quantities of oxygen relative to carbon are thereby formed. If the oxygen energy level were 1 per cent lower, virtually all the carbon inside stars would be processed into oxygen and then much of it into heavier elements still; there would not be enough carbon for life-forms like ourselves to exist[8]. Yet another piece of fine-tuning!

The examples of fine-tuning I have been presenting are illustrations of the Anthropic Principle (see box), which expresses in a formal way that for us to be able to observe the universe, the universe must have developed in a way that enables us to exist (Fig. 3.3). This may sound like a

The Anthropic Principle

A statement of the principle in its weak form is that 'The observed values of all physical and cosmological quantities are not equally probable but they take on values restricted by the requirement that there exist sites where carbon-based life can evolve and by the requirement that the universe be old enough for it to have already done so.'[9]

Stronger statements of the Anthropic Principle have been proposed, for instance 'The universe must have those properties which allow life to develop within it at some stage in its history'[10], which is more speculative in that it not only points out that the universe is this way but implies that it is necessary for it to be so. John Barrow and Frank Tipler have suggested an even stronger form of the principle they call the Final Anthropic Principle which states that

'Intelligent information-processing must come into existence in the universe and, once it comes into existence, it will never die out'[11]. Because they cannot be tested, these more speculative forms are no longer statements of scientific principle; they move into the realm of metaphysics.

Consideration of the Anthropic Principle in any of its forms inevitably raises the possibility of the existence of other universes. Many-universe theories abound among cosmologists[12]. Is, for instance, the universe we know just one of many which have begun from other Big Bangs? How about the possibility suggested by some that regions of our own universe have become 'bubbles' in space-time and form universes on their own, completely inaccessible to us in our universe? Or has statement of the obvious. However, the statement emphasizes just how dependent our existence is on the detailed physics which controls the structure and evolution of the universe, and on the precise nature of the initial conditions which existed in the earliest moments of the universe's existence.

Let us think more about the fine-tuning. Have the particular pieces of fine-tuning I have described been set individually and very precisely at the start of the Big Bang, or have they been 'built in' in a more fundamental way? The Anthropic Principle might suggest that they have been built in. Let me take a comparatively trivial modern example. In whatever part of England I may be, whenever I switch on the radio in my car it is tuned to the music programme Classic FM, even though the appropriate frequency varies from place to place. This might seem to me a remarkable coincidence if I did not realize that my car radio contains a

---

our universe expanded many times from different Big Bangs, each expansion followed by contraction to a 'Big Crunch' (the opposite to a Big Bang), in which case we happen to be in one of many periods of expansion?

From the point of view of our argument here, a relevant question is, 'Given the remarkable structure of our universe and its suitability for life, was it tailor-made for us or is it one of the multiplicity of universes which just happens to fit the requirements?' The concept that there might be an extremely large number of other universes with different characteristics is one which, at least in part, seems to remove the need for our universe to be specially designed or fine-tuned[13]—although it could also be argued that the existence of many universes might provide the means for achieving the required design. But because it is hard to conceive of any ways

through which any other universes can communicate with us, we have no objective means of deciding whether such speculations about their existence have any validity. They also remain in the realm of metaphysics.

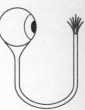

FIG. 3.3 A symbolic picture due to John Wheeler which represents the universe as a self-observing system[14]. The 'tail' of the figure represents the early stages of the universe, the 'body' the development of the universe, in which eventually consciousness emerges, the 'eye', which can observe the universe from which it developed.

clever arrangement which automatically tunes in to the strongest signal on which that programme can be found. The mechanism for fine-tuning has been built in.

Amongst cosmologists the search goes on for a 'Theory of Everything' which can overcome some of the current problems of physics and satisfactorily link all areas of theoretical physics from the extremely small to the very big. It may be that if such a theory—or some closer approach to it—is found, we shall discover that some of the remarkable coincidences of fine-tuning have in fact been built in at a more basic level. For example, a recent theory called 'inflation' which sets out to describe part of the very early expansion in the Big Bang, if it turns out to be correct, automatically guarantees that the universe be 'flat' in the sense we mentioned above.

If indeed elements of the fine-tuning I have described have been built in, they will cease to appear as coincidences. But that does not mean that they are necessarily less remarkable and that we no longer need to be impressed by them; we might, in fact, be more impressed by the original design of the universe which had cleverly built them in.

The science I have been discussing so far has all been concerned with the universe and its evolution—its physics and its chemistry. There is another scientific story concerned with the development of life from very small beginnings to the enormously rich variety of forms in which it appears on Earth. A story equally remarkable (if not more so) could be told about the structure of life, with the many complex and interdependent molecules which make up even the simplest living cell.

We have seen how the universe seems to be fine-tuned with extremely high precision in order for conditions on Earth to be suitable for life. When we now look at conditions on Earth itself, it seems as though there is even more fine-tuning. For example, the average temperature at the Earth's surface and the chemical composition of the atmosphere (the amount of oxygen, carbon dioxide and water vapour) are remarkably near the optimum for the well-being of the forms of life currently present on Earth.

The classic reason for this match between living things

and their environment is that life has adapted itself to the environment of Earth. But, as James Lovelock points out[15], although adaptation is part of the explanation it cannot be the whole story. It cannot explain why, from a wide range of seeming possibilities, conditions so close to the optimum have been chosen. The interdependencies between the physical, the chemical and the biological components seem so strong that Lovelock has suggested that the components of the Earth system work together somewhat as if they made up a single organism, to which Lovelock has given the name of Gaia[16], after the Greek Earth goddess.

This hypothesis has been a powerful one in suggesting new interdependencies and new mechanisms of self-regulation. Some have speculated far beyond the Gaia hypothesis to attribute sentient (if not divine!) qualities to the Earth[17]. There is no justification for such elaboration; we should be content (as Lovelock himself suggests) with the recognition—itself striking enough—that elaborate mechanisms for fine-tuning and for optimization have been built into the basic structure of living systems. Because these mechanisms involve life they are probably more complex even than those to which I have already referred which were built into the universe at the time of the Big Bang. The exploration of these mechanisms will occupy Earth scientists for many years to come.

The story so far

The sketch I have given of the structure and history of the universe is a truly remarkable one—completely beyond our wildest imagination. And I have only given you a small part of the story. A great deal more can be told and even more remains to be found out. Because we are conscious beings, aware of ourselves, searching for meaning, we are particularly interested in how the universe is related to us. Let me try and summarize a few of the relevant points.

☐ Firstly, the universe is a remarkably orderly and consistent whole. The laws which govern its structure, evolution and behaviour can be formulated in ways that are intelligible to us. They are universal. The laws which operate on Earth today also operate ten thousand million light-years away and ten thousand million years removed in time.

☐ Secondly, to provide the rich mix of elements on Earth for life to form and evolve, the whole universe with its long history of billions of years is required.

☐ Thirdly, the provision of the critical conditions for life requires extraordinarily fine-tuning in the initial conditions of the Big Bang and in the basic physics on which the universe is based. As the search for more fundamental theories continues it may be that some of this fine-tuning will appear as an integral part of the basic physics. However, whether introduced as part of the initial conditions or whether included in the basic physics this fine-tuning is part of the universe's fundamental design.

☐ Fourthly, there is the existence of human minds which, so far as we know, are by far the most complex parts of the universe. These minds of ours can investigate and appreciate the universe. We are able to discover in their elegant mathematical forms the fundamental laws which govern its operation and we can appreciate the intricacy and creativity which has gone into its design. Albert Einstein once commented that the only incomprehensible thing about the universe is that it is comprehensible.

☐ Fifthly, the universe is extraordinarily interesting. We cannot fail to be impressed by its complexity, richness, variety and beauty, all of which, incredibly, flow from the basic laws or the initial conditions which appear, in their fundamental form, comparatively simple. Freeman Dyson[17] has suggested a principle of maximum diversity; the laws of nature and the initial conditions are such as to make the universe as diverse and as interesting as possible[18]. We must also be impressed by both the extravagance and the economy of the universe, whether in the range, scale and number of galaxies or in the variety, number, multiplication and interrelatedness of life-forms on Earth.

Our search for perspective and meaning

Where does all this leave us so far as our search for a perspective on God is concerned? We, human beings, need the whole universe; we can feel part of the universe and to some degree can understand the design and operation of the universe. Paul Davies, an astrophysicist who has written several books on physics and cosmology, provides in his book *The mind of God*[19] a detailed review of the history of the universe and concludes:

Through science we human beings are able to grasp at least some of nature's secrets. We have cracked part of the cosmic code. Why should this be, just why Homo sapiens *should carry the spark of rationality that provides the key to the universe is a deep enigma. We who are children of the universe— animated stardust—can nevertheless reflect on the nature of that same universe, even to the extent of glimpsing the rules on which it runs. How we have become linked into this cosmic dimension is a mystery. Yet the linkage cannot be denied. What does it mean? What are human beings that we might be party to such privilege? I cannot believe that our existence in this universe is a mere quirk of fate, an accident of history, an incidental blip in the great cosmic drama. Our involvement is too intimate. The physical species* Homo *may count for nothing, but the existence of mind in some organism on some planet in the universe is surely a fact of fundamental significance. Through conscious beings the universe has generated self-awareness. This can be no trivial detail, no minor byproduct of mindless purposeless forces. We are truly meant to be here.*

Let me remind you of two questions I asked in Chapter 1. 'Does bringing in the idea of a Designer add insight and explanation to life?' was one question, and 'Supposing there is a Designer, what can we learn about him and what is his relationship to us?' was the other.

Regarding the answer to the first question, after the quotation I have just given we shall not be surprised to find that Paul Davies writes, 'Personally I feel more comfortable with a deeper level of explanation than the laws of physics.' However, he is not sure 'whether the use of the term "God" for that deeper level is appropriate'[21]; nor is he sure that 'this postulated being who underpins the rationality of the world bears much relation to the personal God of religion'[21]. Paul Davies is not alone in wanting a deeper level of explanation[22]. Stephen Hawking hints at it in the closing paragraph of his book *A brief history of time*[23] when he looks forward to the possible discovery of a complete theory of the universe which would enable there to be a fuller discussion of 'why it is that we and the universe exist'. 'If we find the answer to that,' he writes, 'it would be the ultimate triumph of human reason—for then we would know the mind of God.'

Davies and Hawking when writing of God are thinking of the Great Mathematician who thought up and gave realization to the basic equations underpinning the structure of the universe. A mathematical role for God has been around a long time; Plato is said to have remarked that God geometrizes continually and fifty years ago the popular science writer Sir James Jeans described God as the Great Mathematician[24]. Such a role for God does not, however, move us very far in our quest for meaning. As Stephen Hawking has commented, 'One can of course define God as the answer to the question Why does the universe bother to exist?, but that does not advance one very much unless one accepts the other connotations that are usually attached to the word God'[25]. Hawking goes on to say that his position on that is open.

This latter point made by Hawking—that if we are going to think of God at all, it only makes sense to do so in a context much larger than that of a great mathematical designer—is key to answering the first question[26]. Because what we are about is the quest for meaning, the first question may be answered positively if, instead of using the word 'Designer' for God's activity, we think of God as the Purpose-maker.

44

We can now move on to the second question: 'Supposing there is a Purpose-maker, what can we say about him and his relationship to us?' We have already emphasized the enormous intelligence necessary to conceive a universe of such fantastic design with its interlocking interdependencies. The Purpose-maker is orderly and precise; reliable and consistent. He knows about beauty and elegance; economy and extravagance are also words that we have used about his design.

What about his relationship to us? We have seen the evidence that the universe has been designed with beings like ourselves in mind. We have also seen that we possess the capability both to understand and to appreciate something of the grand design, even, perhaps most surprising of all, its mathematical basis. We can also take in something of its beauty. All this is possible because we have minds, consciousness and self-awareness. These properties are not easily included in our current scientific descriptions; I argue in Chapter 6 that their understanding represents one of the greatest challenges to our contemporary science.

Since we possess these characteristics it is, I believe, very reasonable to argue that they should also be characteristics of the Purpose-maker; indeed it would seem to me unreasonable to conceive of a Designer who did not at least possess them to the degree we have them. When Hawking and others talk of the 'Mind of God' they are not, I suggest, thinking merely of an enormous computer, but of a conscious entity. In so doing they are, perhaps inadvertently, attributing personal qualities to God. The Purpose-maker must possess the qualities of consciousness—of being a Person.

If there is this likeness between us and the Purpose-maker, if the Purpose-maker is a Person who has developed the universe with human beings in mind, then we are bound to ask whether there is the possibility of forming a relationship with him. After all, the only way personal qualities can be expressed is through relationships. Although part of the creation, we are sufficiently like the Purpose-maker really to be able to appreciate his design. Because we also are creative we can speculate about its nature and at least in some sense share in the sheer delight which must have been associated with its creation. The Bible's way of expressing the relationship is to state in its first chapter that we are created in the image of God[27].

If the objective question of whether and how the universe was designed were the only reason to bring the idea of God into our thinking, whether or not there is a Designer behind the design would merely be a matter for academic debate—a suitable topic for after-dinner conversation in Oxford common-rooms. But our exploration of the answer to the question 'Supposing there is a Designer, what is he like?' ends with the speculation that the Designer or Purpose-maker, having characteristics of a person, might be known by us and that human persons might be able to have a relationship with him.

If it really is the case that we can in some real sense get to know the Designer of the universe, that is something very big and exciting indeed. From our scientific exploration we are led to the need for religious exploration. Hugh Montefiore writes, 'Natural theology[28] only permits us to view God from afar. We are, as it were, out of range of his voice, too distant to recognize more than his bare outline. That is why we need so badly his further self-disclosure.'[29] And William Temple, Archbishop of Canterbury, wrote sixty years ago: 'Natural Theology ends with a hunger for that Divine Revelation which it began by excluding from its purview.'[30]

Footnotes

1   In quantum physics there is a fundamental limit to the accuracy to which time can be described. This Planck time is 10^{-43} seconds.

2   J. Gribbin and M. Rees, *Cosmic Coincidences*, Black Swan, 1991, p 18.

3   Gribbin and Rees *loc. cit.*, p 92.

4   B.G. Levi, 'COBE measures anisotropy in cosmic microwave background radiation', *Physics Today*, 45, 1992, pp 17–20.

5   R. Penrose, *op. cit.*, p 444.

6   R. Penrose, *The Emperor's New Mind*, OUP, 1989. In Chapter 7 Penrose points out the difference between the initial singularity such as the Big Bang and a final singularity which would occur if, for instance, the universe were to recollapse into what has become known as the Big Crunch. That final situation would be one of very high entropy.

7   Gribbin & Rees, *loc. cit.*, p 244.

8   Gribbin & Rees, *loc. cit.*, p 246.

9   J.D. Barrow & F.J. Tipler, *The anthropic cosmological principle*, OUP, 1986, p 16.

10   Barrow & Tipler, *ibid*, p 21.

11   Barrow & Tipler, *ibid*, p 23.

12   See Barrow & Tipler, *ibid*, for a detailed discussion of many-universe theories.

13   The philosopher John Leslie, in his book *Universes*, Routledge, 1989, considers that it might provide an alternative—although, in his view, not a likely alternative—to the hypothesis that God is real and the designer of the one universe which we know.

14   Adapted from Angela Tilby, *Soul: an introduction to the new cosmology—time, consciousness and God*, BBC Education, London, 1992, p 47.

15   J.E. Lovelock, *The ages of Gaia*, OUP, 1988.

16   J.E. Lovelock, *Gaia: a new look at life on Earth*, OUP, 1979.

17   A review of views of the Gaia hypothesis is given by L. Osborn 'The Machine and the Mother Goddess: The Gaia Hypothesis in Contemporary Scientific and Religious Thought', *Science and Christian Belief*, 4, 1992, pp 27–41.

18   P. Davies, *The mind of God*, Simon and Schuster, 1992, p 173.

19   P. Davies, *loc. cit.*, p 232.

20   P. Davies, *loc. cit.*, p189.

21   P. Davies, *loc. cit.*, p 191.

22   See for instance H. Montefiore, *The probability of God*, SCM Press, 1985.

23   Bantam Press, 1988.

24   Sir James Jeans, *The mysterious Universe*, CUP, 1945, p 122.

25   S. Hawking, 'In defence of *A brief history*', *Cambridge Review*, **Vol 113**, pp 16–17, 1992

26   A point made by John Leslie, *loc. cit.*, Chapter 8.

27   Genesis 1.26.

28   'Natural theology' is concerned with what we can learn about God from study of the natural world.

29   H. Montefiore, *loc. cit.*, p 177.

30   W. Temple, *Nature, Man and God*, Macmillan, 1934, p 306.

PART 2
Where Can We Find God?

Four arguments are often raised against the possibility of God: that the increasing scope of science has removed the need for God as an explanation; that scientific descriptions are the only valid way of looking at the world; that chance and chaos argue against a consistent design, let alone a Designer; and that the idea of God in control of the world denies human free will. The next four chapters address these problems.

4 A God Who Hides

Truly, you are a God who hides himself.
ISAIAH 45:15

In the last chapter, I described the evidence which leads to the view that the universe has been made with humans in mind. I also reasoned that the Purpose-maker behind the universe must possess personal qualities, such that we can reasonably explore the possibility of a relationship with him.

But if such a Purpose-maker exists, why is he not more evident, why does he not make his presence in the world more felt? That is a question which people have been asking from the very beginning of human existence. To many, God, if he exists, appears remote. How can a God who has made such a vast universe have any interest in us, we ask? But is God really hard to find, or are we looking in the wrong places? Let us ask the question, 'Where are we looking for God?'

Hiding in the beginning?

First, there is a general belief that God has a special role in initiating the universe; we might therefore expect to find signs of his activity at the beginning of things. When astronomers began to publicize their belief that the universe had started with a definite beginning in the Big Bang, many religious people saw that as evidence of God the Creator bringing the universe into existence. But how clear is that 'beginning'?

In this context I want to refer to Stephen Hawking's book *A brief history of time*[1]. It is a remarkable book, not only for its content but also because of its remarkable popularity; it has already sold over six million copies in hardback. This popularity has no doubt been aided by interest in Stephen Hawking as a person, in his remarkable struggle against a crippling disease. But, by popular standards, it is far from an easy read. The fact that people want to buy it demonstrates a widespread and deep interest in the universe, its origins and the search for meaning.

The references to God in Hawking's book have raised a lot of interest. Hawking comments on the trouble he has received from theologians and philosophers but felt he 'could hardly leave God out of a discussion of the origin of the universe'[2]. His discussion of the origin of things centres around the very beginning of the Big Bang; he gets round the problem of the initial singularity, the definite beginning, by what he calls a 'no boundary' condition; in Hawking's theory (see box) there is no actual beginning.

Hawking's theory of 'no beginning'

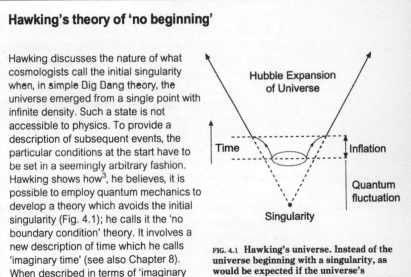

Hawking discusses the nature of what cosmologists call the initial singularity when, in simple Big Bang theory, the universe emerged from a single point with infinite density. Such a state is not accessible to physics. To provide a description of subsequent events, the particular conditions at the start have to be set in a seemingly arbitrary fashion. Hawking shows how[3], he believes, it is possible to employ quantum mechanics to develop a theory which avoids the initial singularity (Fig. 4.1); he calls it the 'no boundary condition' theory. It involves a new description of time which he calls 'imaginary time' (see also Chapter 8). When described in terms of 'imaginary time' the initial singularity is no longer present. There is no boundary, and therefore no beginning.

FIG. 4.1 **Hawking's universe. Instead of the universe beginning with a singularity, as would be expected if the universe's expansion is extrapolated back in time, the universe arises from a quantum fluctuation as an already finite expanding region which is then amplified by 'inflation'[4].**

What implications does Hawking's new, clever, very technical theory have? If the universe has no beginning, what place is there for a creator? he asks.

If the only role for a creator is to appear, light the blue touch-paper right at the beginning of the Big Bang and retire, then he may not be required. But a creator with such a comparatively trivial role would be a trivial creator. As John Polkinghorne points out in discussion of Hawking's theory[5], our interest in God as creator is not so much concerned with temporal origin (*how* did things begin?) but with ontological origin (*why* is there anything at all?). In the last chapter of his book Hawking raises exactly that question when he writes concerning a possible unified theory of the universe that 'it is just a set of rules and equations. What is it', he asks, 'that breathes fire into the equations and makes a universe for them to describe?'[6] I shall return to these questions later in the chapter.

Hiding in the automatic mechanisms?

A second place where God seems to hide is in the mechanisms which govern the operation of the universe. Let us return to Paley's analogy of the person walking on a heath who found a watch. Given the watch, how do we find the watchmaker?

Clearly a watchmaker cannot be found within the mechanism of the watch itself. However, supposing that he maintains an interest in his watch, he might be expected to be available from time to time to wind it up, to adjust it to the right time or to clean and maintain it—unless, that is, the watch is sufficiently elaborate and accurate not to need any such attention.

Even early watch- and clockmakers aimed at automatic adjustment and maintenance. For instance, in the palace of Versailles there is a clock dating from the eighteenth century which records not only the minute and the hour, but the day, month, year and phase of the moon, with mechanisms that take account of all the necessary adjustments for leap years and the like for many centuries ahead.

The better constructed and more complete the timepiece, the less need there is for the watchmaker to be available for maintenance or adjustment. The more elaborate and perfect the watch, the less likely therefore are we to meet the watchmaker. Indeed, the ideal timepiece is one which needs no attention at all, in which case the watchmaker need never appear.

I have spent many years designing and building scientific equipment for artificial satellites. Such equipment needs to be extremely robust and reliable. Hands-on maintenance is not normally possible; the cost of visits by the space shuttle is prohibitive. In such a design, the space-equipment designer needs to consider all possibilities of failure, to build in redundancy—so that the device can still operate if part of it goes wrong—and to include back-up systems wherever failure is likely. Automatic means of correcting for failure need to be provided. The technical description for such equipment is 'fault-tolerant'. The Voyager spacecraft, for instance, which explored the outer solar system, Jupiter, Saturn, Uranus and Neptune, continued to function for many years of travelling through space. Its construction was extremely reliable and fault-tolerant.

Modern computing equipment has a similar requirement. The circuitry built into a large silicon chip can be so complex that complete testing of it is not possible; some failures would be difficult if not impossible to identify. A degree of fault tolerance is therefore essential. With fault-tolerant equipment that is properly designed, there is no need to appeal to the designer for maintenance or adjustment. It should continue to function according to its specification for as long as its design life. After that, it can be discarded and replaced.

In the last chapter I detailed a number of examples of incredibly precise 'fine-tuning' associated with the early development of the universe, and I suggested the possibility that fundamental mechanisms which would automatically guarantee the fine-tuning might exist—very remarkable automatic control mechanisms right at the heart of the universe's design.

In a different sphere, the human body is an excellent example of fault-tolerant equipment. The body's biochemistry has elaborate mechanisms to combat or eliminate disease built in. A substantial degree of redundancy has been provided in the brain and other parts of the body so that the body can still function even if large parts are damaged or removed. It also possesses a remarkable ability to adapt to a changing environment.

The human body is one example among many of fault tolerance in biological systems. Others are described by the Oxford biologist Richard Dawkins in *The Blind Watchmaker*,[7] the book in which he expounds what he believes to be the great capability of the mechanism of natural selection for adaptation and adjustment. He argues that nothing further is required to explain the development of the living world, and that, having found the mechanism, there is no need to invoke the existence of a designer; the mechanism of natural selection can be considered as 'the blind watchmaker'.

However, the fact that we understand some of the mechanisms of the working of the universe or of living systems does not preclude the existence of a designer, any more than the possession of insight into the processes by which a watch has been put together, however automatic these processes may appear, implies that there can be no watchmaker.

Anselm of Canterbury in the eleventh century introduced a definition of God as 'the greatest conceivable being'.[8] That definition implies that God must be not only the great designer but the greatest possible designer. He would design a universe entirely reliable, precise, self-consistent, without need for continuous adjustment and with a high degree of fault tolerance. We would not therefore expect God to have to appear to push the system back into line, or to correct for unforeseen errors. It is not surprising that the universe appears so complete and self-contained. If we are looking for dramatic evidence of God's special activity in the normal operation of the universe, we are perhaps looking in the wrong place or with the wrong kind of expectation.

A further point before moving on; in emphasising the orderliness of God's normal activity in the universe, I do not wish to rule out the possibility of special 'miraculous' events which appear to be outside the normal scientific order, although I believe such events to be comparatively rare. I shall consider such events particularly in Chapter 13.

Hiding in the scientific story?

The third place where God seems to hide is an extension of the second; he seems to hide in the scientific story itself. Traditionally, it has been assumed that God is responsible for events for which there seems to be no other explanation. Early scientists would invoke God as the explanation of phenomena for which their science could not account. One of the most frequently quoted examples concerns Isaac Newton who, having discovered that the law of gravity accounted neatly for the rotation of the moon about the Earth, found difficulty in explaining the spinning of the Earth on its axis. He wrote to the Master of his Cambridge college, Trinity, 'The diurnal rotation of the planets could not be derived from gravity but required a divine arm to impress it on them.' Because this 'God' provided a convenient explanation for the gaps in human understanding, he came to be described as 'the God of the gaps'.

As science has advanced and provided more and more explanations, the need to account for the unexplained in terms of God receded. Although we commonly continue to describe as 'acts of God' some unpredictable natural phenomena—the lightning strike, the volcano or the earthquake—we feel that their unpredictability is merely a consequence of our scientific ignorance; they are probably not unpredictable in principle. Similarly, in the medical sphere, it is often thought that God is only in demand as the healer when medical solutions have failed. The 'God of the gaps' has become smaller and smaller as scientific knowledge has grown and as the gaps have lessened. Chance and 'chaos' are now found to give suitable descriptions of many fundamental processes in science (see Chapter 6) and an underlying picture of order been discovered in unpredictable systems—no clear 'finger of God' to be seen there, either.

We are still a long way from filling in all the details of the scientific story, and the scientific enterprise goes on unabated. At the most fundamental level, the search for a Grand Unified Theory continues, with the object of tying together all the elementary forces and particles into one all-embracing scheme.

At other levels, the power of the physical and mathematical tools available to the scientist is continually demonstrated, as phenomena in the physics laboratory (see box), in the cosmos or in living matter move from the territory of the unknown to that of the directly perceived.

Electron spin and the Dirac equation

The work of Paul Dirac in 1928 is a particularly elegant piece of physics which illustrates the power of the scientific approach in integrating theory and observation and which also demonstrates the deep orderliness and consistency in the structure of the natural world.

From the earliest days of spectroscopy, it has been known that atoms, when heated in flames, give off radiations at characteristic wavelengths. We are all familiar, for instance, with the bright yellow light given off by sodium atoms when sodium is present in a fluorescent lamp or when common salt is put into a flame. If such radiation is broken down into its components, instead of a rainbow effect with each band of radiation merging into the next, every band corresponds to one wavelength only, showing up as a separate (discrete) line on the spectrum.

In the early years of this century, one of the triumphs of the new quantum mechanics was its ability to provide an explanation for the existence of these discrete spectral lines. In 1913, Niels Bohr, the Danish physicist, set up a simple model of the atom in which the energy levels of an electron in an atom could be described by three numbers, called quantum numbers (Fig. 4.2). The numbers are like the components of an address—for instance the town, the street and the house number—which enable any given home to be located. Spectral lines arise from electrons 'jumping' between these energy levels, emitting radiation in the process.

It turned out, however, that three numbers were not enough to describe some of the complications of observed spectra. In 1925, Wolfgang Pauli, an Austrian physicist, suggested a fourth quantum number, called the 'spin' quantum number. It seemed that the electron was spinning on its axis and that the direction of the spin axis could be oriented in two ways commonly described as 'up' and 'down'. Going back to the example of the postal address, if all houses in the town are divided into two apartments, it is necessary to add 'upper' or 'lower apartment' to the address if post is to reach its correct destination.

This idea of electron spin and the four quantum number worked well as a means of labelling quite complicated spectra and of explaining the ordering of elements in the periodic table. There was, however, no good theoretical basis for it—the concept of 'spin' just had to be tacked on to explain the observations.

Around the same time, in the late 1920

New scientific discoveries continue to confirm scientists in their belief in the existence of a deep orderliness and consistency in the natural world—an orderliness I have already emphasized when pointing out that the physics which applies in the laboratory turns out to be the same physics which is observed by astronomers to apply, far

Paul Dirac, a brilliant young English physicist working in Cambridge, was trying to devise a new wave equation for the electron. Schrödinger's equation of 1926 was fine in that it agreed with the new ideas of quantum theory, but it did not satisfy Einstein's theory of relativity. While still only twenty-six years old, in 1928, Dirac solved the problem. To everyone's delight and surprise, the new Dirac equation required the electron to 'spin' by just the amount required to explain the observations of spectra. No longer had the fourth quantum number to be tacked on as an unsatisfactory appendage; it became a natural consequence of the mathematical description.

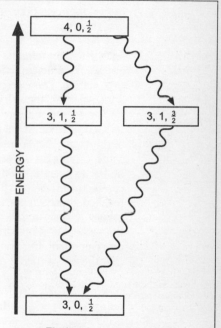

FIG. 4.2 The first few energy levels of a sodium atom. The numbers by each level are the quantum numbers n, l and j, numbers which are employed to describe the electron configuration in each energy level. Transitions between the energy levels which result in the emission of light are shown. The yellow light at wavelengths of 0.5890 and 0.5896 micrometres, characteristic of emission from sodium atoms, results from transitions from the first two excited levels (3, 1, $^1/_2$ and 3, 1, $^3/_2$) to the lowest energy level (3, 0, $^1/_2$).

removed in space and time, in the most distant parts of the universe. It is this belief in order and consistency which enables the scientist to formulate principles and give them the status of scientific law. In fact, the whole of science depends on it. And not only the whole of science, but our ordinary day-to-day living depends on that fundamental consistency and order more than we readily realize—for instance, if the law of gravity could not be relied upon, ordinary life would be impossible.

Although the scientific picture is still far from complete and no end is yet in sight for the scientific enterprise, the scientist's aim remains to explain all, and everything seems at least in principle amenable to scientific investigation and explanation. There seems no reason to doubt that eventually a full scientific picture of the universe can be achieved.

But where, if anywhere, in this description is there room for God? Although we recognize the inadequacy of the 'God of the gaps', there continues to be a tendency to fall into the same trap and in our search for 'explanation' to allow God to be the explanation where science currently fails. If God is confined to those parts of the universe science has not yet reached, those supporting belief in God are supporting a lost cause. Earlier in the chapter, I presented an example of this—Stephen Hawking, having found the 'no boundary' description of the beginning of the Big Bang, concluded that there was therefore no need for a creator.

If scientific laws are taken as a successor to the creative power of God, however, we are misunderstanding their nature. Because scientific laws are so powerful and can be applied so usefully, we give them a high status. But they are purely descriptions (albeit in most cases very good descriptions) of the world as the scientist sees it. In no sense do scientific laws make things happen. An apple, in falling to the ground, we say, is 'obeying the law of gravity'; but the law of gravity does not cause the apple to fall; it describes what normally occurs when an apple is severed from its branch.

The place where we can find God, the 'greatest conceivable being', is not in the gaps not covered by these descriptions. God is not just active in those areas which science cannot explain, as if science were an alternative to God. Instead, our science *is* God's science. He holds the responsibility for the whole scientific story. Our problem is that our thoughts about God are far too small.

Let us return again briefly to Paley's watch. Automatic and accurate though it is, it still needs a source of energy to keep it going. This could be an extremely long-life battery, the movement of the wearer's wrist, or light from the sun impinging on solar cells and so generating electrical power. Whatever it is, the source of energy is an essential part of the design and therefore the concern of the designer.

How is the universe kept in being? It is sometimes said that it 'maintains itself', whatever that may mean. In which case, if there is a great designer, he must have provided for that self-maintenance. But to be kept in being is more fundamental than mere maintenance. It does not make much sense to conceive of a God who created the universe without also being active in keeping it in being; we need to think of God not only as the great designer but as the source of that which keeps the universe in existence.

The Christian picture of God as presented in the Bible is of one who is intimately concerned with his universe, one who, in fact, continually sustains it[9]. God is then the great sustainer through whose continued moment-by-moment activity the whole show of the universe continues. To use Stephen Hawking's phrase, it is God who is 'breathing fire into the equations'.

I have been arguing that if we are going to think of God at all, it only makes sense to have the biggest possible view of him, the greatest perspective. This is not a new idea. The picture of God as designer, creator and sustainer of the universe is one which accords well with that found in Hebrew thought in the Old Testament, where often the closeness of God to his creation is emphasized[10]. We also find it in Christian thought in the New Testament where we are presented with a picture of Jesus as the one who 'sustains all things'[11] and 'in whom all things hold together'[12]. For Jews and Christians alike, learning about the universe (even the very limited universe they knew) was a step in learning about God.

The scientific story and the faith story

I have been presenting God as the author of the 'scientific story' which scientists are striving to elucidate. In science we are describing what God is doing in his sustaining work. In the words of the sixteenth-century astronomer Johannes Kepler, we are 'thinking God's thoughts after him'. The remarkable order, consistency, reliability and fascinating complexity found in the scientific description of the universe are then reflections of the order, consistency, reliability and complexity of God's activity.

But God, presented in this way, is still obscured by the universe and remains remote. Can we find God within the universe? If so, in what way? Russian cosmonauts have visited outer space and reported that they cannot find him there. We have no expectation of coming across God in a spaceship or of bringing him into the focus of an earthbound telescope.

There are, however, ways in which we can find God within the universe; I will be exploring some of them in subsequent chapters. One way is to look into the 'scientific story' and see God's thoughts. Another way I will call the 'faith story': the description and interpretation of events when viewed with the 'eye of faith'—in other words, in the context of a relationship with God.

Let me introduce this by referring to a story from the life of Jesus[13]. Some of the Jewish religious leaders came to Jesus and asked him to show them a sign from heaven so that they could believe in him. Jesus refused to do anything special for them, but pointed out to them their knowledge of signs for weather forecasting—that a red sky in the evening precedes fair weather but a red and overcast sky in the morning is followed by stormy weather. He then chided them for not being able to interpret 'the signs of the times'. In other words, their meteorological science was effective, but they were severely lacking in their appreciation of God's activity in the world. In particular they failed to recognize who Jesus was and the significance of the message which he had brought. They had not got very far with the 'faith story'.

Christians, encouraged by reading the Bible, in particular

Paul's Journey to Rome (Acts 27)

Scientific story	Faith story
Very severe north-east gale	All 276 lives on board saved
Cargo overboard	Publius' father healed on Malta
Shipwreck on Malta	Christianity comes to Malta

learning of the words and actions of Jesus, and encouraged also by the experience of other Christians down the centuries, talk of God's providence, of God's care for people. They expect to see signs of God's action in their day-to-day lives. As scientists strive to make sense of the 'scientific story', so Christians strive to make sense of the 'faith story'. 'What is God saying to me through this event?' they ask. Just as scientists have learnt to look for order and consistency in the 'scientific story', the expectation of believers in God is that there is also order and consistency in the 'faith story'—that God is trustworthy in relationships as well as in the laws of the universe.

Let us take as an example (see box) the journey of Paul from Jerusalem to Rome recorded in the Acts of the Apostles[14]. The 'scientific story' includes a storm, not unusual in the autumn in the Mediterranean, and a shipwreck on the island of Malta. A scientist present would doubtless have been able to fit the facts together into a satisfactory description—the 'scientific story'. Paul and Luke (the author of Acts) also saw a 'faith story'. They saw the events as fitting into a particular divine plan.

'Is not this view from the perspective of faith an illusion?' the sceptical scientist may argue. After all, the events in question are following nothing but the ordinary process of scientific law. But the scientist has no right to say, 'It is *nothing but...*' The existence of the 'scientific story' in no way rules out the validity of the 'faith story'; both stories have an equal claim to be considered. The two stories are complementary; they are views from different perspectives and told largely in different language.

The complementary nature of different stories was a particular theme often expounded by Charles Coulson, a distinguished scientist who during his lifetime held university chairs in mathematics, in physics and in chemistry. He illustrated it from the draughtsman's plans of a large building, which take a variety of forms—plans of different floors, various elevations, plans for the electricity and the plumbing, views in perspective and so on[15]. Although there may be common features between some of them, each of them is complete in itself and serves its particular purpose. Each drawing is necessary, but since there is only one building, the different drawings are bound to be complementary to each other. Although when we consider the whole of reality, including God, the connections between our different experiences are harder to elucidate than is the case with the drawings of a building, we can look for the same sort of complementarity.

I have just discussed the importance of consistency in the interpretation of the scientific view—a quality which, I have argued, stems from the characteristics of the creator and sustainer of the universe. The more deeply the natural world is understood, the more consistent does the scientific position appear. Consistency is also important in the view of faith. Just as the scientist achieves considerable satisfaction in seeing how events in the physical world fit together in terms of scientific law, so Christians will find support for their faith as they are able to interpret the events around them in terms of a divine plan. The Christian who is also a scientist will therefore be looking for a *double consistency* in the interpretation of events.

But even though the stories are complementary, if God is the author of both, we are bound to ask the question: how can God fit together in a consistent way both the 'scientific story' and the 'faith story'. This seems to become more of a problem as we think about the implications of our own freedom as human beings. How can God allow for that as well?

I shall be addressing this question in more detail in Chapters 6 and 7. The point I want to make here is that, in our thoughts about God, we constantly make him too small; we imagine him to be just a little bigger than ourselves. If God is to be really God, he must be very great indeed—'the greatest conceivable being' is the description I have been using. He is the designer-creator-sustainer of our universe and, for all we know, of other universes too. Although we are made in God's image and therefore can relate to him and appreciate some of his attributes, we are extremely limited by comparison. We too can design and create but in an incomparably smaller way. He is incomparably greater than ourselves and incomparably greater than our thoughts about him[16].

If God really is that big, I suggest that we can assert that God is both big enough and clever enough to solve simultaneously two interrelating jigsaws—the scientific jigsaw and the faith jigsaw—and so ensure at the same time consistency in the 'scientific story' and significance in the 'faith story'. This God cannot be squeezed into the gaps in our knowledge, but sustains every way of looking at the world.

Footnotes

1   S. Hawking, *A brief history of time*, Bantam Press, 1988.

2   S. Hawking, 'In defence of *A brief history*', *loc. cit.*

3   S. Hawking, *A brief history of time*, p 133ff.

4   From David Wilkinson, *God, the Big Bang and Stephen Hawking*, Monarch, 1993.

5   J. Polkinghorne, 'The mind of God?', *Cambridge Review*, **113**, 1992, pp 3–5.

6   S. Hawking, *loc. cit.*

7   Longmans, 1986

8   This definition was introduced by Anselm of Canterbury in the eleventh century in connection with one of the classic 'proofs' of God's existence. Anselm called God 'the greatest conceivable being', and argued on logical grounds that because what exists in reality is greater than what exists only in thought, it is necessary, if God is the greatest conceivable being, for him to exist in reality as well as in thought.

9   Psalm 90:1–2.

10   For instance in the great hymn to creation, Psalm 104.

11   Hebrews 1:3

12   Colossians 1:17

13   Matthew 16:1–4

14   Chapters 27 and 28

15   C.A. Coulson, *Science and Christian Belief*, OUP, 1955, p 67.

16   Isaiah 55:8–9

5 Explaining Things Away

Only wholeness leads to clarity.
FRIEDRICH VON SCHILLER

In the last chapter I mentioned the common view that God provides an alternative explanation to that of science—that the 'God of the gaps' can be brought in to provide explanations where science fails. I pointed out the inadequacy of this view from both the religious and scientific standpoints, and introduced the idea that different descriptions can be complementary.

However, the view that, if a scientific explanation of a given event is available, all other descriptions are superfluous is a deep-seated one. In this chapter, therefore, I want to pursue the validity of different levels of explanation, mostly taking illustrations from within science itself.

One of the most powerful tools available to the scientist is that of analysis or breaking things down into component parts. Examples of the process readily come to mind. Atomic physics, for instance, is all about the particles making up atoms; nuclear physics is all about the components of nuclei and the forces that hold them together. Molecular biology has developed from an understanding of the properties of molecules such as DNA which form the basis of living material. The science of chemistry is based on knowledge of the make-up and structure of the molecules forming different compounds and materials—for instance, the strength and the high refractive index of a diamond are due to the arrangement of electrons within the elementary diamond crystal, the blue colour of the sky is due to sunlight scattered preferentially at the shorter (blue) end of the visible spectrum by nitrogen and oxygen molecules in the atmosphere—and so on.

The analytical approach is also effective in less conventional scientific disciplines. The classical experiments of the Russian physiologist Pavlov on dogs, for instance, showed how the process of learning could be understood in terms of stimulus and response. Psychologists and behavioural scientists in their turn look at the way human behaviour is related to genetic inheritance, childhood environment and the influence of different relationships.

Because analysis is such a powerful tool in science, it is often argued that it is all-powerful, and that, having described the component parts, the interactions between them and the way they fit together, there is nothing more to be said. The whole is then nothing but the sum of the parts.

So strong is this analytical instinct that the all-embracing power of analysis has become with some a tenet of belief; reductionists are people who believe in reductionism. If only we knew enough, the reductionists[1] argue, everything could be reduced to elementary particles, and elementary forces. The whole of science and of human experience is then nothing but the sum of billions and billions of elementary parts. Reductionism, it appears, has the power to explain everything away—anything that cannot be described in terms of components does not exist.

The falsity of the reductionist approach may be illustrated by taking the example of a painting. A chemist would describe it in terms of various chemical substances distributed in certain patterns over the canvas; a physicist might go into the spectral properties of the pigments; other scientists might be able to determine its age or the origin of the materials of which it is made. None of these descriptions has any relevance to the beauty or the artistic message of the painting. In no way has that message been 'explained away' or made superfluous by the detailed analytical descriptions.

In using the illustration of the painting, descriptions taken from different disciplines have been involved, and it has been rather easy to show the weakness of the

The Orsay experiment [2]

Pairs of photons (particles of light) leave excited calcium atoms (atoms which have been stimulated by energy input) in opposite directions (Fig. 5.1a). Before arriving at detectors, which may be many metres apart, they pass through polarization analyzers which only allow photons with a particular direction of polarization to pass through. These analyzers can be oriented in any one of three directions at 120° to each other. The orientation of the analyzers is changed continuously and randomly. The signals from the detectors record the detection or non-detection of the photons.

In accordance with the predictions of quantum mechanics, it is found that (1) whenever the analyzers are set in the same direction, the detectors give identical signals, i.e. the photons are either both detected or both blocked by the analyzers, and (2) whenever the analyzers have different settings the detectors give identical signals only one quarter of the time.

The surprising feature of the prediction is that the probability of one of the photons passing through its analyzer and being detected depends on the setting of the other analyzer and the probability of the other photon being detected. Thus the quantum-mechanical description treats both photons together throughout the whole event until they have both been detected, even though the detectors may be many metres apart. No single set of instructions could be given to the photons as they leave the emitting atoms which could achieve this result. The formal proof

of this is due to J. S. Bell in 1964 and is known as Bell's theorem.

Another way of thinking about this experiment which may be helpful pictures men instead of photons and gates instead of polarization analyzers (Fig. 5.1b). Men leave a central location in pairs, running in opposite directions towards two sets each of three gates, numbered respectively 1, 2 and 3. As each man arrives at the gates he will find only one gate open (chosen at random and constantly changing); he has to choose whether or not to go through the gate. He is unable to see his partner or the gates his partner is encountering as he makes his choice.

The gate which is open is indicated to the observer on a display panel. The observer also notes whether or not each man chooses to go through the open gate on his side. As a large number of pairs of men reach the gates, the observer finds that (a) whenever the same-numbered gate is open simultaneously on the two sides, the two men make identical choices—they both go through or they both fail to go through—and (b) whenever different-numbered gates are open on the two sides, the two men are much more likely to make different choices (in fact, they make different choices three-quarters of the time).

Think for a few minutes about the findings of the observer. To achieve the first result—that identical choices are made by the men whenever the same numbered gate is open—it seems necessary that before they leave the central location, the men should agree on the choices they will make, depending on which gate they find open. However, no set of instructions which can achieve this first result can also achieve the second, namely that when different gates are open the men will make the same choice only one quarter of the time.

To achieve the second result as well as the first, some collusion is necessary between the men when they reach the gates and discover which of the gates is open. No such collusion is allowed by the experiment—so the conclusion that the men behave as if they are part of one system, although they are widely separated, is inevitable.

FIG. 5.1 **The Orsay experiment**

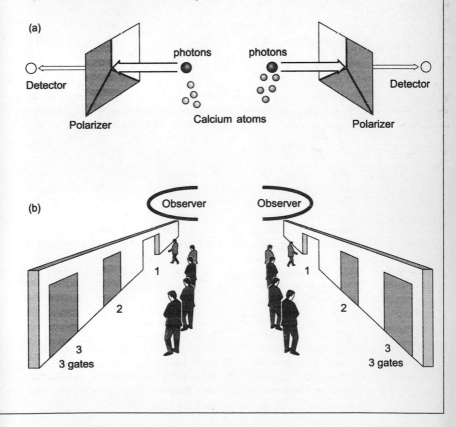

reductionist argument. It is also interesting to realize, and important to emphasize, that even if we confine ourselves to the realm of physical science, where the analytical approach is most effective, it is not all-powerful. If we imagine the whole to be made up just of the sum of the parts, important areas of science itself (not to mention other areas of experience and knowledge) will be missed or badly misunderstood. Let me demonstrate this by taking a couple of examples from physics.

The first example comes from quantum mechanics, which governs the behaviour of the very small particles which make up atoms. According to quantum mechanics, the location and behaviour of elementary particles can never be completely defined; they have to be expressed as probabilities rather than certainties. Further, particles initially belonging to a particular system need to be considered together even when they may have moved so as to be far apart.

This quantum description can come up with surprising results which tend to go against our intuition. A particularly telling example is demonstrated by experiments carried out by Professor Aspect and his colleagues at the Orsay Laboratory in Paris (see box). In these experiments, pairs of photons (particles of light) emitted by calcium atoms are examined. Their behaviour cannot be explained by treating the photons as separate entities, even though during the experiment they may be many metres apart without any possibility of influencing each other. Even though there are only two particles in this system, the whole is more than the sum of each particle acting separately.

The second example comes from thermodynamics. Two different gases are present in the two compartments of a box (Fig. 5.2(a)) If we make a film of the movements of the individual molecules of the two gases just after the partition separating the gases has been removed (Fig. 5.2(b)), the film will show the molecules colliding with each other and with the container walls. All motions of the gas molecules are entirely consistent with Newton's laws of motion. Gradually the two gases diffuse throughout the container until they are completely mixed.

Suppose now the film were to be run backwards. Again the molecular motions would appear entirely consistent with Newton's laws. From the point of view of these laws applied to individual particles there is no way of deciding when the film is moving forwards and when it is moving backwards. However, we know that gas molecules do not in reality move so as to separate the two kinds of molecules into the two ends of the container. There is a physical law which states that in such circumstances, disorder tends to increase with time: the law of increase of entropy. The process of mixing of gases such as I have described is not reversible. In fact, it is one of the processes in physics which enable a direction to be given to time[3].

On viewing the two films, we would have no difficulty in choosing the one in which time is moving forward. However, the basic laws of motion are equally valid for time going

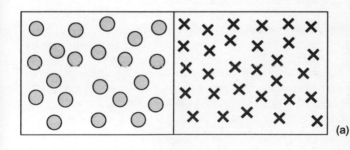

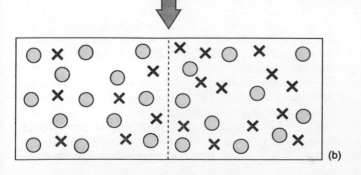

FIG. 5.2 A container containing 2 gases (molecules labelled O and X); (a) in separate compartments, and (b) after the partition between the compartments is removed.

forwards or backwards. By considering individual molecules, the concept of entropy or a preferred direction to time will not emerge. To realize these concepts, new ideas appropriate to the behaviour of very large assemblies of molecules have to be introduced and new properties defined. Thus even in basic physics the whole is more than the sum of the parts.

I turn now to a much more complicated system—the human brain. Some understanding of its basic mechanisms can be made by comparing the brain to a computer with its logic circuits (its hardware) and its programs (its software)—although, with perhaps a hundred thousand million nerve cells, called neurons, it is much larger and more complex than any computer yet constructed. Can we suppose that the behaviour of the human brain could be reduced to nothing more than the behaviour of an extremely complex super-computer? What about, for instance, the properties of consciousness or self-awareness and the ability to make free choices, not possessed by computing hardware of human construction?

Francis Crick, the Nobel prizewinner who with James D. Watson discovered the double helix structure of DNA, has spent recent years working on the brain and the problem of consciousness. He has put forward what he calls the 'Astonishing Hypothesis'[4], namely that

'You', your joys and your sorrows, your memories and ambitions, your sense of personal identity and free will, are in fact no more than the behaviour of a vast assembly of nerve cells and their associated molecules.[5]

It is indeed an astonishing hypothesis; it is reductionism with a vengeance! How we interpret such a statement depends on what is meant by the phrase 'no more than'. If it means that we should not expect to find extra material called 'consciousness' or 'self-awareness' which somehow pervades the brain without being part of it, I would readily agree. But if it means that the properties of consciousness, self-awareness and free choice could somehow be explained away if we knew enough about the operation and organization of the nerve cells—I suspect that is in fact what Crick means—then I am bound to disagree.

Scientific investigation of the links between the behaviour of the brain's neurons and conscious behaviour is an essential part of the search for more understanding both of the way the neurons operate and interconnect and of what we mean by consciousness. Such investigations look hard for links between properties of the whole, such as self-awareness, and the microstructure of individual parts[6]. But we cannot argue that properties such as consciousness are illusory because they do not appear in the individual computer elements (or neurons) which make up the brain, any more than we can argue that entropy is illusory because it cannot be found in the individual molecules of gas in a container. Neither can we argue that our free choices are not really free, without also denying our self-awareness[7].

Properties such as consciousness and free will are sometimes described as 'emergent'—they emerge, perhaps gradually, at some time during the development of the complex structure of the brain. None of the links we may find, however, between the microstructure and these emergent properties, will 'explain away' these properties of the whole. I shall return to consider some fundamental problems underlying the science of the brain in the next chapter.

What I have been doing in this chapter is giving examples of hierarchies of description[8]. Descriptions of objects or of events can be given at different levels, each employing the language and thought forms appropriate to its level. The different levels may be within one particular intellectual discipline (for instance, physics or psychology), or they may belong to very different disciplines.

For instance, let us look at a sacramental meal, when a company of worshipping persons take bread and wine together. It can be described in terms of the basic biology of the growing process of the wheat or the grape, or in terms of the chemistry of yeast or fermentation through which wheat is turned into bread or grapes into wine, or perhaps in the framework of the agriculture and economy of cereal and wine production. It might also be described in terms of the social and behavioural patterns involved in human association and relationships and in the development of religious experience.

A further description might be given concerning the portrayal of the sacramental meal in art—by a Leonardo da Vinci or a Michelangelo—or its association with music over the centuries. Then, of course, there is its description in a Christian context as an aid to faith. There are connections between these different descriptions, but they are in no way mutually contradictory. If one description seems particularly adequate, the validity of a description at a different level is not called into question. It is important to recognize that no particular description can explain things away or preclude the possibility of another description.

Progress in science is made both through exploration of the component parts of a system and also through standing back and putting different ideas together. The big leaps in scientific thought have been taken by those who have taken a broad and integrated view. So, then, if we turn to the material and experience of faith, it is entirely proper that these should be analyzed by the scientific tools at our disposal; such analysis can be helpful in leading to critical understanding. But it does not 'explain away' the reality of faith or of religious experience.

In the realm of faith, putting alongside each other different parts of the whole can be especially valuable. An underlying theme of this book is the wholeness of God's revelation as seen both in the natural world explored by science and in his special revelation in religious experience. I shall return particularly to this theme in Chapter 9 and again in Chapter 15, where I believe we shall see again that the whole is greater than the sum of the parts.

In the meantime, I shall consider those areas of science where consistency and predictability appear to break down, and try to find some underlying patterns.

Footnotes

1   Believers in reductionism. Professor D.M. MacKay has nicknamed reductionism 'nothing-buttery'.

2   Further details of the experiment can be found in N.D. Hermin, *Physics Today*, Phoenix, 1985, pp 38–47.

3   For more details see R. Feynmann, *The Character of Physical Law*, BBC Publications, 1965, Chapter 5.

4   Francis Crick, *The Astonishing Hypothesis, the Scientific Search for the Soul*, Simon and Schuster, 1994.

5   Francis Crick, *loc. cit.*, p 3.

6   A.R. Peacocke, in *God and the New Biology*, Dent, 1986, expounds this in some detail.

7   Professor D.M. MacKay has argued (for instance in *Brains, Machines and Persons*, Collins, 1980) that freedom of choice is a logical consequence of self-awareness.

8   A.R. Peacocke, *Creation and the World of Science*, OUP, 1978. See also R. Feynmann, *op. cit.*, p 125.

6 Chance, Chaos and Order

Chaos umpire sits, and by decision more embroils the fray by which he reigns; next to him high arbiter Chance governs all.
JOHN MILTON

If it is argued that God can be found in the orderly processes of the natural world, what about those processes which appear disorderly or to be governed by chance? Do they argue against the existence of God? In this chapter I return to the 'scientific story' and look particularly at some of the developments this century emphasizing the involvement of chance or 'chaotic' processes in the natural world, which at first sight seem to deny meaning to the universe.

Chance and the scientific revolution

From the mid-seventeenth century until around the mid-nineteenth century, the physics introduced by Isaac Newton reigned supreme. In Newtonian mechanics everything could be calculated with unlimited precision; its crowning success had been its description with remarkable accuracy of the orbits of the planets. The movement of any object at any time in the future could, at least in principle, be predicted precisely, provided its present position and movement were known. The precision and the deterministic flavour of Newtonian physics has had an enormous influence, not just on the way we think about science but on the the way we think more generally.

But around the middle of last century, as the science of thermodynamics was developed, cracks began to appear in this basic Newtonian structure. Then, at the beginning of this century, a revolution began to occur in our physical understanding. It was discovered that the very small particles within atoms do not obey Newtonian mechanics. A new sort of mechanics, quantum mechanics (mentioned in the last chapter), was introduced which was not nearly so deterministic. In quantum mechanics, prediction of the future behaviour of atomic systems is in terms of probabilities rather than of certainties (see box). Principles of uncertainty are built into the basic structure of physics.

All this seemed disturbing at the time. At the beginning of the first chapter I recalled that Albert Einstein, even though he had played a large part in the discovery of quantum mechanics, felt uncomfortable with the new ideas. He felt that behind the probabilistic accounts of quantum mechanics there should be some more deterministic descriptions. Basic reasons are now known why these cannot be provided in the framework of quantum mechanics. Chance and uncertainty are now universally accepted

---

Quantum mechanics and probabilities

Take an elementary particle, such as an electron, a constituent particle of all atoms. According to quantum mechanics it behaves like a wave and to describe its position or its motion a wave equation is used. Because a wave spreads over a region of space, it is not possible to say exactly where the electron is located— only the probability of different locations can be provided. The motion of the electron (to be more exact, its momentum) cannot be precisely known either. That there is uncertainty in our knowledge of both the position and the momentum of an electron is expressed in the Heisenberg Uncertainty Principle, named after its discoverer.

If a light wave is incident on a glass surface, such as a window, some is reflected and some is transmitted—you see reflections from the glass surface, but you can see through it as well. If an electron 'wave' encounters a barrier, for instance a metal surface, again some of the wave is reflected and some is transmitted. But has the electron as a particle been reflected or transmitted? The physicist cannot say. What can be provided from the 'wave mechanics' of quantum theory is the probability of the electron being reflected and the probability of it being transmitted.

in science as fundamental to descriptions of the behaviour of the very small. Some uncertainty is thereby introduced into descriptions of the behaviour of much larger systems, made up of these very small components.

Poincaré's work on chaos

When Isaac Newton published his *Principia* in 1686, he had applied the newly discovered inverse square law of gravitation to the movement of systems involving two bodies—the sun and a planet or a planet and a moon. Such equations for two bodies can be solved exactly: solutions to any degree of precision can easily be realized. But for more complicated cases in which three or more bodies are involved exact solutions are not available. The standard procedure is to employ what is called perturbation theory; beginning from a simple first approximation (such as the solution for a two-body system), the perturbing effects of the third body are added successively to higher and higher degrees of approximation. Finally it is necessary to prove rigorously that the procedure converges to a well-determined limit—that as it is carried out more and more times, it approximates more and more closely to a particular value. Many famous names are associated with the development of Newtonian mechanics during the eighteenth and nineteenth centuries, for instance those of Euler, Lagrange, Laplace, Hamilton and Poincaré.

Such perturbation methods work well in a wide range of cases in which successive approximations converge to a solution whose value can be obtained more and more precisely as the number of approximations is increased. But there are some cases for which the perturbation method does not converge—where a single final solution cannot be reached. It was Poincaré in 1903[1] who recognized that the actual solutions in such cases might be highly dependent on the initial conditions. He wrote as follows:

A very small cause which escapes our notice determines a considerable effect we cannot fail to see, and then we say that the effect is due to chance. If we knew exactly the laws of nature and the situation of the universe at the initial moment, we could predict exactly the situation of the same universe at a succeeding moment. But even if it were the case that the natural laws no longer had any secret for us, we could still only know the initial situation approximately. If that enabled us to predict the succeeding situation with the same approximation, that is all we require, and we should say that the phenomenon had been predicted, that it is governed by laws. But it is not always so; it may happen that small differences in the initial conditions produce very great ones in the final phenomena. A small error in the former will produce an enormous error in the latter. Prediction becomes impossible, and we have the fortuitous phenomenon[2].

That was in 1903. Poincaré had recognized chaotic situations—situations, where from infinitesimally different starting points very different outcomes can result.

Chance processes are also important in biology, which has seen its own revolution this century. It began about forty years ago with the discovery of the structure of DNA, the molecule which carries the genetic code and which, with its double-helix structure, possesses a remarkable ability to reproduce. The total genetic code for a human being, known as the genome, contains about a thousand million bits of information. Small alterations in the code—mutations—can arise through chance variations during the copying process or through accidental changes resulting, for instance, from the background of natural radiation which is present to a greater or lesser extent everywhere. Such mutations may, in some cases, be damaging to the living system. But they can also provide the raw material for development; the continued reshuffling of the DNA pack enables some of the potential for development within living matter to be explored[3]. Chance processes are fundamental to the richness and fruitfulness of our universe.

The discovery of 'chaos'

We have seen how classical Newtonian physics has been superseded in considering the behaviour of atomic systems, but it still applies perfectly well to physics at larger scales. What has only been appreciated recently, however—during the past twenty or thirty years in particular—is that Newtonian mechanics itself is not as deterministic as was thought. There had been hints of this earlier; attempts to apply Newton's mechanics to more complicated systems (see box) demonstrated the difficulty of obtaining precise solutions in some situations. But it was the advent of the electronic computer with its capacity for high-speed calculation which showed the extent of what is called chaotic behaviour.

The word 'chaotic' is perhaps an unfortunate choice as it suggests something completely random and unstructured. In this context it must be understood as a technical term describing a system whose behaviour is extremely dependent on the initial conditions from which the system started—so dependent, in fact, that after a short time it becomes essentially unpredictable. Let me explain in a little more detail how such behaviour arises and give a few examples[4].

It was a meteorology professor, Edward Lorenz at the Massachusetts Institute of Technology, who in 1961 accidentally came across 'chaos' and brought it to the notice of the scientific world[6]. He had written down the simplest equations he could think of to describe convection in the atmosphere—a set of three equations involving three variable quantities—and he wanted to calculate how atmospheric motions evolved with time by using these

The Lorenz attractor

The three simple Lorenz equations set up as a model for convection in the atmosphere involve three variables, x, y and z. Using these equations computer calculations can be made from different starting conditions of the evolution of the variables over time. The results when plotted on a three-dimensional diagram describe a pattern which is known as the Lorenz attractor. A cross-section of the attractor is shown in Fig. 6.1. By tracking the evolution of the variables from starting conditions which are close together, the degree of divergence (and therefore the degree of chaos) can be ascertained. Some trajectories are much more chaotic than others.

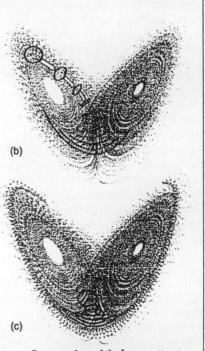

(b)

(c)

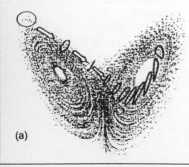

(a)

FIG. 6.1 Cross-sections of the Lorenz attractor showing how solutions to the equations evolve from different ensembles of initial states.
(a) shows little divergence,
(b) more divergence and (c) 'chaotic' solutions
(after T.N.Palmer[5])

equations. Working with one of the early electronic computers which, by today's standards, was extremely slow and primitive (it could perform a mere 60 operations per second; modern computers employed for weather forecasting are one hundred million times faster!) the calculations took many hours of computer time. To continue a particular computer run from where he had left off, numbers had to be typed in by hand.

On a particular occasion, Lorenz had taken the values reached by his three variables in the middle of a computer run and used these values to start another long calculation on the machine. The first part of the new calculation was therefore repeating the second part of the earlier run—or so he thought. But when he compared the two calculations, the results were not the same. They started together but gradually diverged until they bore no resemblance to each other. Could the computer be at fault, he wondered?

In a flash Lorenz realized what had happened. He described it to a science writer, James Gleick[7]. There had been no malfunction. The problem lay in the numbers he had typed when starting off the second run. In the computer's memory six decimal places were stored; one of the numbers was 0.506127. On the print-out, to save space, just three appeared: 0.506. Lorenz had entered the shorter rounded-off numbers, assuming that the difference—one part in a thousand—did not matter. It was surely too crude a model for such a small difference to be of any consequence. But the difference, although small, turned out to be highly significant; Lorenz quickly realized that he had stumbled across something important.

Most of Lorenz's career since then has been devoted to the study of the atmosphere as a chaotic system—he is still working on it, thirty years later. Half jokingly, chaos in the atmosphere is sometimes referred to as 'the butterfly effect', taken from the title of a lecture given by Lorenz in 1979: 'Predictability; does the flap of a butterfly's wings in Brazil set off a tornado in Texas?'

Does Lorenz's work mean that weather forecasting far into the future is doomed? The answer is partly yes; partly, because it seems that a complex system like the atmosphere is partly chaotic (see box). Even if we could observe the state of the atmosphere all over the globe much more accurately than at present (in other words provide much more precise initial conditions for the computer forecasting model), forecasts of detailed weather conditions would be possible at most some two or three weeks into the future. But forecasts of the average weather or the climate, at least in some parts of the world, may be possible much further ahead. And, despite the frightening complexity of the whole climate system, we also have good reason to expect that useful predictions can

---

Chaos with a simple pendulum

For a bob swinging around in a circle at the end of a string, the frequency of natural oscillation (the frequency with which the bob swings when allowed to swing freely) is given by a simple expression[9]. Suppose that an arrangement is set up such that the point from which the pendulum is suspended is moved along a line in an oscillatory way at a forcing frequency close to the pendulum's natural frequency of oscillation (Fig. 6.2). At some values of the forcing frequency the behaviour of the pendulum is regular and predictable and not very dependent on the precise way the driving force is applied. But at other periods close to resonance (when the forcing frequency equals the natural frequency of oscillation), the pendulum behaves in a 'chaotic' way; it is then extremely sensitive to minute variations in the driving force. Although the motion is confined to a particular region of the diagram, it is compounded of many kinds of movements: some clockwise, some anti-clockwise, some mainly above the x-axis, some mainly below. Transitions between

these different kinds of movement occur not only randomly but discontinuously as a function of the initial conditions[10].

Suppose that at some stage of the motion very precise details are available of the motion of the bob and the forcing motion. Can the bob's subsequent motion be predicted? To begin with there would be good correspondence between predictability and observation. But as time goes on the predictability and the observation will diverge, the time before substantial divergence occurs being called the predictability horizon. If the initial conditions are more accurately defined, the predictability horizon will move away, but not by much. Roughly speaking, the predictability horizon increases proportionally to the number of decimal places in the definition of the initial conditions. If, for instance, four decimal places (0.01 per cent) accuracy in the initial conditions enables prediction for one minute, twelve decimal places or one part in a million million would provide for three-be made of the likely climate change due to human activities[8].

Examples of chaos

I must not give the impression that it is only very complex systems such as the atmosphere which exhibit chaos. That is not the case; many comparatively simple systems can also be chaotic in their behaviour. Take, for instance, a set of perfect billiard balls on a perfectly smooth table making perfect collisions with each other and with the perfect cushions (Fig. 6.3). If the cue ball is struck by the cue, how sensitive to the exact stroke of the cue are the later positions

minute prediction. Very rapidly, therefore, prediction becomes virtually impossible. Another way of describing this behaviour is to say that a property of chaotic systems is that neighbouring solutions diverge exponentially from one another.

For a system to be likely to exhibit chaotic behaviour it is not necessary for it to be particularly complex. The key factor is that the governing equations must be non-linear[11]. In the case of the simple pendulum

the expression for its period is only linear to the extent that the sine of the angle of the string to the axis can be approximated by the angle itself. As the angle becomes larger, this approximation becomes less accurate; it is this feature that provides the non-linearity. Physicists, of course, like linear equations because they are easier to solve; they look for linear equations to provide approximate descriptions of any phenomenon or problem with which they are faced. But, in reality, nearly all systems in nature are non-linear and therefore fulfil one of the conditions for chaotic behaviour.

FIG. 6.2 **Chaos shown by a conical pendulum with a string of length 10 cm. The diagrams show plots of the bob's motion on a horizontal plane, the scale being in centimetres.**

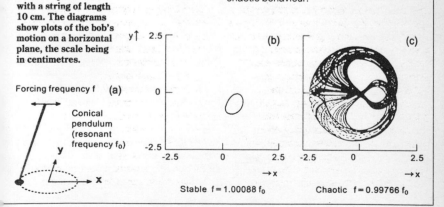

Forcing frequency f (a)

Conical pendulum (resonant frequency f_0)

(b)

Stable f = 1.00088 f_0

(c)

Chaotic f = 0.99766 f_0

FIG. 6.5 The variation of fish population with a variable called the 'boom and bustiness' showing a region of regular variation, a chaotic region and a number of bifurcation points. The black region on the right of the diagram is full of structure and contains a very large number of bifurcations[12].

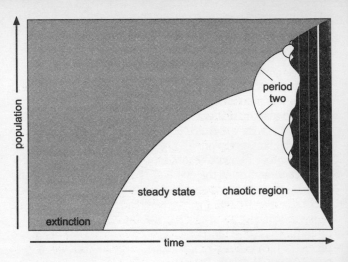

James Clark Maxwell on bifurcations

James Clark Maxwell, the theoretical physicist best known for his work in the 1860s in which he integrated electricity and magnetism and showed that light waves are electromagnetic in character, was aware of the potential of bifurcations even in classical systems. He also anticipated their application in very different fields. He wrote:

In all such cases there is one common circumstance—the system has a quantity of potential energy, which is capable of being transformed into motion, but which cannot begin to be so transformed till the system has reached a certain configuration, to attain which requires an expenditure of work, which in certain cases may be infinitesimally small, and in general bears no definite proportion to the energy developed in consequence

thereof. For example, the rock loosed by frost and balanced on a singular point of the mountain side, the little spark which kindles the great forest, the little word which sets the world a-fighting, the little scruple which prevents a man from doing his will, the little spore which blights all the potatoes, the little gemmule which makes us philosophers or idiots. Every existence above a certain rank has its singular points: the higher the rank, the more of them. At these points, influences whose physical magnitude is too small to be taken account of by a finite being, may produce results of the greatest importance. All great results produced by human endeavour depend on taking advantage of these singular states when they occur[13].

of the balls? The sensitivity is surprising. If the position of
the balls one minute after the stroke is to be accurately
predicted, effects as small as the gravitational attraction of
a electron moving at the edge of the galaxy have to be taken
into account[14]! Another example is provided by something
as simple as a pendulum (see box).

FIG. 6.3 **The motion
of billiard balls is
very dependent on
the size and
direction of the
stroke from the
cue.**

An important feature of many chaotic processes is the
existence of what are called bifurcations. Imagine a perfectly
smooth ball at the top of an upturned U in a perfectly smooth
tube (Fig. 6.4). The smallest disturbance, which need involve
no expenditure of energy, is sufficient to cause the ball to
move one way or the other down the tube. The top of the tube
is a bifurcation point for the ball. Because of the extreme
sensitivity of a system to even the smallest fluctuation at a
bifurcation point—the point of choice—it is impossible to
predict which subsequent path the system will follow (see
box). A typical chaotic system may include very large numbers of such bifurcation points, providing an enormous range
of possibilities of choice. Studies of the variation of animal or
insect populations with different variables provide good
examples of systems with many bifurcations (Fig. 6.5).

Before leaving the subject of chaos, I would like to bring
you a couple of examples of order seeming to come out of
chaos. The first is an example from meteorology, not of the
Earth's atmosphere but of Jupiter. Because of the colours of the
gases which make up Jupiter's atmosphere, the details of the
motions of its atmosphere can easily be seen from the television
pictures taken by the Voyager spacecraft which passed by
Jupiter in 1979. Much of the motion is highly turbulent and
chaotic. But standing out in this turbulent flow are a number of
smoother features. One of them, the Great Red Spot, is large—
about 15,000 km in diameter. It is surrounded by many smaller
rapidly changing eddies from which it obtains the energy to
keep it going[15]. It is a remarkably stable feature, having been in
existence for at least the 300 years since it was first seen by
Robert Hooke in 1664 through one of the early telescopes. It is a
remarkable example of an orderly and stable system existing
in the midst of flow which is otherwise largely chaotic. Its
existence encourages us to look for stable and predictable
components in the flow of our own atmosphere.

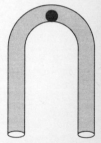

FIG. 6.4 **A smooth
ball at the top of an
upturned U in a
smooth tube
illustrates a
bifurcation point.**

Another rather spectacular example comes from chemistry. Some thirty years ago a Russian chemist named Boris Belousov happened to mix in a beaker a cocktail of not-very-nice chemicals: sulphuric acid, potassium bromate, cerium sulphate and malonic acid. You would imagine that reactions between such chemicals would proceed apace, leading eventually to equilibrium—uniform distributions of whatever chemicals were the result of the reaction. That, however, was not the case. He noticed that oscillations were produced in the concentration of cerium and bromide ions formed such that the colour of the mixture in the beaker changed from blue to magenta and back again several times per minute. These oscillations would continue for hours[16]. Belousov had discovered one of what are now known as 'clock reactions'. At the time no one believed him: they thought he was not a very good chemist—he could not even mix his chemicals correctly! Years went by and it was not in fact until after Belousov's death that his work was accepted.

Reactions are going on in the chemical cocktail which under some conditions lead to regular oscillations. Under other conditions the behaviour is chaotic, or a mixture of regular and chaotic changes. Belousov's reaction is an example of the sort of behaviour which can occur in a system far from equilibrium. Many more such examples are now known. Non-equilibrium dynamics is an area of intensive study which has been particularly pioneered by the Nobel Prizewinner, Ilya Prigogine. Because of their complexity, situations which are far from equilibrium or which are irreversible have not been attractive ones for scientific study; physicists, on the whole, have shied away from them. However, in a classic book *From Being to Becoming*[17], Prigogine explores the exciting possibilities opened up by such seemingly unpromising situations. Chaos and order prove to be closely interlinked[18].

Chaos and determinism

What implications does our understanding of chaos have for Newtonian determinism? Do we have to throw it out of the window? No, we do not. Considered from the point of view of

classical physics, events in the chaotic systems we have
been describing are as predictable in theory as they are in
any Newtonian system. What we have been at pains to point
out is the extreme difficulty of any attempt at such a
calculation. Prediction of the behaviour of a simple system
when in chaotic mode, even for a relatively short time ahead,
may involve virtually complete knowledge of the whole
universe. Even if that complete knowledge were available, a
further difficulty, which has been pointed out by Roger
Penrose[19], is that there are fundamental problems with the
actual mathematical computation of the future state of a
system. If, therefore, scientists talk of 'deterministic chaos',
they are not suggesting that there is any practical possibility
of the chaos actually being determined; it is just that in
principle, in a classical Newtonian sense, 'deterministic'
remains an accurate—though not very useful—description.

But if quantum mechanics is also included in our
description of events, as soon as the specification of the
initial conditions required for prediction involves details,
say, of the movement of individual electrons, the Heisenberg uncertainty principle (see box in Chapter 7) becomes
relevant. We come up against an inability not only in
practice but in principle to specify with adequate precision
the initial conditions. This means that prediction of the
future behaviour of very many large-scale systems, even
for a relatively short time ahead, also becomes impossible in
principle.

Chance, chaos and God's activity

Having outlined some of the background to the rôle of
chance and chaotic processes in the scientific description of
things, let us now turn to consider the implications posed by
chance and chaos for the way in which we think of God's
activity in the world.

First let us look at chance. In doing so I am bound again
to emphasize the fundamental and positive role which is
played by chance processes in the structure of all parts of
the universe[20], from the very big to the extremely small. In
Chapters 2 and 3 I referred to random processes in the early
history of the universe, assisting in the development of

galaxies and even present very close to the beginning of the Big Bang itself. Moving to the other end of the scale of things, chance processes occur at the atomic level where they govern, for instance, the decay of radioactive nuclei. There are also chance processes which play a large part in the science of genetics.

Not only do considerations of chance and probability play a large part in our modern scientific description, be it in physics or biology, they also permeate other parts of our experience. Our daily lives are filled with 'chance' occurrences. We are bombarded with statistics about the probability of being born with various defects, of particular sorts of crime, of death from various causes, and so on. Insurance against improbable events is big business.

Because chance is so important, the question is often asked how God can be involved in such a random universe. The French geneticist Jacques Monod in his book *Chance and Necessity*[21] has publicized the view that chance has ruled God out. Monod comments, concerning the origin of life, 'Our number came up in the Monte Carlo game.' Richard Dawkins in *The blind watchmaker*[22] argues that chance processes have provided a firmer basis for Darwinian evolution, and believes that his expositions do away with any need for God[23].

But it is essential to realize that 'chance' does not make things happen. As Donald MacKay[24], a scientist concerned with information theory, especially related to how the brain works, and the biologist Arthur Peacocke[25] have cogently argued, chance and probability, although properly part of a scientific description, are not causes of events any more than any other scientific description or law can be said to have causal properties. Further, although the scientific description of some event (the 'scientific story' of Chapter 4) may involve chance and probability, it does not follow that the complementary theological description of the same event in terms of God's activity (the 'faith story' of the same chapter) involves chance in the same way. In this theological sense, Einstein was right to say, 'God does not play dice'!

In the last chapter I exposed the 'reductionist' traps into which it is so easy to fall; I mentioned those into which physicists have often fallen when suggesting that the whole of physics is contained in, or can be reduced to, a few fundamental equations. Monod and Dawkins are falling into the same trap in biological science. As Arthur Peacocke explains[26], it cannot be argued that, because of the success of molecular biology, biological mechanisms are 'nothing but' physics and chemistry. Neither can it be said that, because of the success of evolutionary theory, all biology can be reduced to a single evolutionary mechanism. Further, the existence of evolutionary mechanisms in the development of the universe or in the development of life in no way rules out the possibility of God; these are some of God's mechanisms of creation (see Chapter 4). John Hapgood, the Archbishop of York and a trained scientist, in replying to Richard Dawkins comments, 'Dawkins has done excellent work in evolutionary theory by demonstrating how complexity can arise out of simplicity. But he has moved from science to scientism in making this the key to his universe, even to the point of ridiculing God for not conforming to his pattern.'[27]

Turning now to chaos, the same general arguments apply. Chaos does not make things happen. It is a fundamental feature of the scientific description, but a description in terms of chaos theory in no way rules out other descriptions, in particular theological descriptions in terms of God's activity.

But our knowledge that the universe is full of systems that exhibit chaotic behaviour has brought some important new perspectives to our thinking about the world and how God might be acting in it. I want to mention three[28].

☐ First, we realize that the scientist's capacity to predict the future is very much more limited than we previously thought.

☐ Secondly, our study of chaotic systems shows that complicated behaviour can emerge as a consequence of simple non-linear interactions between a few components.

It is not just that the behaviour is more complicated, but resulting from such interactions completely new kinds of behaviour with new forms of order can emerge which could not be deduced from knowledge of the individual components. Chapter 5 demonstrated the inadequacy of the simple reductionist view that complex systems can be fully understood by breaking them down into their component parts. Our understanding of chaotic systems further knocks reductionism on the head.

☐ Thirdly, chaos provides a mechanism for enormous leverage (a small movement at one end of a lever leads to a large movement at the other end) from the very small to the very big. In living systems, with similar effect to that of the operation of chance processes, chaos provides for access to novelty. Computers are now powerful enough that some of the complex behaviour of living systems involving both chance and chaotic processes can be simulated in computer models; even in the computer models novel behaviour appears to emerge[29]. In an article in the *Scientific American*, J.P. Crutchfield and his co-authors speculate that ideas from chaos may assist in thinking about processes in the brain. They write[30]:

Even the process of intellectual progress relies on the injection of new ideas and on new ways of connecting old ideas. Innate creativity may have an underlying chaotic process that selectively amplifies small fluctuations and moulds them into macroscopic coherent mental states that are experienced as thoughts. In some cases the thoughts may be decisions, or what are perceived to be the exercise of will. In this light, chaos provides a mechanism that allows for free will within a world governed by deterministic laws.

This interesting speculation is one we need to examine more thoroughly. I shall do so in the next chapter where I address briefly the question of what we know about the workings of the brain, the existence of human consciousness and the nature of free will, in order to link it, by analogy, to God's action in the world.

Footnotes

1   Ian Stewart, in *Does God play dice?*, Blackwell, 1989, gives a popular description of Poincaré's work.

2   From an essay on 'Science and Method', quoted by James Gleick in *Chaos*, Heinemann, 1988, p 321.

3   For a popular account of the way in which chance processes can be used in evolutionary development see R. Dawkins, *The blind watchmaker*, Longmans, 1988. Dawkins' account is eminently readable although some would argue that he overstates the power of Darwinian natural selection; his detailed worked examples are drawn more from computer simulations than from real biology. Further, he argues without any basis that the existence of the Darwinian mechanism rules out existence of a Deity.

4   Easily readable accounts of examples of chaos can be found in *The New Scientist guide to chaos*, ed., Nina Hall, Penguin Books, 1991.

5   T.N. Palmer, *Bull. Amer. Met. Soc.*, **74**, 1993, pp 49–65.

6   E.N. Lorenz's book, *The essence of chaos*, University of Washington Press, 1993, is an eminently readable account of the development of the subject of 'chaos', with many illustrative examples.

7   James Gleick, *Chaos*, Heinemann, 1988.

8   For more details see my Bakerian lecture (John Houghton, 'The predictability of weather and climate', *Phil. Trans. R. Soc. Lond. A (1991)*, **337**, pp 521–72) and my book *Global Warming: the complete briefing*, Lion Publishing, 1994.

9   The period is $2\,(l/g)^{1/2}$ where l is the length of the string and g is the acceleration due to gravity.

10   This system has been described by J. Lighthill, 'The recently recognized failure in Newtonian Dynamics', *Proc. R. Soc. Lond. A (1986)*, **407**, pp 35–50 and by D. Tritton, 'Chaos in the swing of a pendulum', *New Scientist*, 1986, pp 37–40.

11   An equation such as $y = ax + b$ is linear because a graph plotting y against x gives a straight line. Examples of non-linear equations are $y = ax^2 + b$ or $y + xy = ax + b$; plots of y against x for these equations would not be straight lines.

12   Work due to Professor Robert May reported by J. Gleick *loc. cit.* pp 70, 74.

13   Quoted by I. Prigogine & I. Stengers, *Order out of chaos*, Fontana Paperbacks, 1985, p 73.

14   See J.P. Crutchfield *et al.*, 'Chaos', *Sci. Amer.*, **255**, 1986, pp 38–49.

15   For more detail see R. Hide, 'Jupiter and Saturn: Giant magnetic rotating fluid planets', *The Observatory*, **100**, 1980, pp 182–193.

16   More details of this and other such reactions in Stephen Scott, 'Clocks and chaos in chemistry', *New Scientist*, 2 December 1989, pp 53–59.

17   W.H. Freeman, 1980; also I. Prigogine & I. Stengers, *Order out of chaos*, Fontana Paperbacks, 1985.

18   A.R. Peacocke, in *Creation and the World of Science*, Chapter 3, gives examples of the appearance of order-through-fluctuations in physical and chemical systems.

19   R. Penrose, *The Emperor's New Mind*, OUP, 1989, pp 220ff.

20   For an expansion of the role of chance see A.R. Peacocke *loc. cit.* and D.J. Bartholomew,

God of Chance, SCM Press, 1984.

21   English edition, Collins, 1971.

22   Longmans, 1986.

23   R. Dawkins, 'A scientist's case against God', *The Independent*, Monday 20 April 1992, p 17.

24   D.M. MacKay, *Science, Chance and Providence*, OUP, 1978.

25   A.R. Peacocke, *Creation and the world of science*, Clarendon Press, 1979.

26   A.R. Peacocke, *God and the New Biology*, J.M. Dent, 1986.

27   John Hapgood, 'Science and God: the Archbishop's reply', *The Independent*, Monday 4 May 1992, p 17.

28   J.T. Houghton, 'New Ideas of Chaos in Physics', *Science and Christian Belief*, 1, pp 41–52, 1989.

29   Roger Lewin, *Complexity*, Phoenix Paperbacks, 1993.

30   Crutchfield *et al., loc. cit.*

7 God's Freedom and Ours

In his heart a man plans his course, but the Lord directeth his steps.
PROVERBS 16:9

In Chapter 4, I presented two stories, the 'scientific story' and the 'faith story', which I suggested were complementary stories, often told in very different language. I also suggested that God is both big enough and clever enough to ensure at the same time consistency in the 'scientific story' and consistency and significance in the 'faith story'.

Because the two stories are concerned with the same events in the world, they are bound to be related and it makes sense to ask how they tie together and how each of the stories can illuminate the other. Further, it is in our nature to want to explore and to ask further questions about how God runs the universe. In this exploration, I believe an understanding of the 'scientific story' can add important theological perspective to our view of God. Our experience of the 'faith story' will inevitably be influenced by what we know of the complementary 'scientific story'. And in its turn our appreciation of the 'scientific story' can also be enhanced by reflecting on the 'faith story'.

Two more 'stories'

Much of the later chapters of the book will be concerned with how the 'scientific story' and the 'faith story' are related. But before moving on I want to introduce two further stories which are concerned with how our freedom of action as conscious human beings fits in with the scientific description of the processes which occur within the brain.

Our conscious experiences and choices we can call the 'I-story' (I think, I feel, I hope, I choose and so on), while the detailed physical, chemical and biological processes occurring in the brain can be called the 'brain-story'[1]. The problem of how these two 'stories' are related is one to which I referred briefly in Chapter 5; it is one of the major challenges of current science.

My reason here for pursuing how these two further stories are related is because of the parallel which we can draw between God's freedom to act and our freedom[2]. There is a basic human belief that (although our choices are limited by the framework of space and time in which we exist and also constrained to a considerable degree by our upbringing and our experience), we have real freedom of choice and action. I have also argued that God is active in the world on a moment-by-moment basis, sustaining everything. Unless we have some understanding of how our own freedom of action in the world is achieved, we cannot expect to make sense of God's sustaining activity.

Before I describe some current scientific thinking about consciousness, it is important to realize that consciousness and free will are closely linked. We do not consider that living creatures that are not conscious are free to choose or to act in the way that humans are. It is because we are conscious and can make deliberate conscious choices that we possess some freedom of action[3]. Further, even if we believe the physical processes in our brain to be deterministic, our freedom of action is not illusory. Fundamental arguments confirm what to most of us in any case seems self-evident, that our freedom of choice and action are real[4].

Human consciousness and scientific laws

The human brain is sometimes compared to an electronic computer. Both can carry out logical processes and calculations, although for arithmetical computations, computers are enormously faster. What seems to be different about the human brain is its ability to think (although computers can simulate some of the processes associated with thinking), to feel and, above all, its property of consciousness or self-awareness.

It is argued by the strong school of what is called Artificial Intelligence (AI) that we could expect a human-built computer which is sufficiently large and complex to exhibit the ability to think, as well as showing character-istics of consciousness or self-awareness. Brains would then be just computers—albeit very complex and remarkable ones—made of meat! But is that an adequate view? There are many questions we might like to ask about it:

Suppose we were presented with an advanced artificial brain which appeared to exhibit human qualities, would we be able to decide to what extent it possessed human qualities?

Could we unequivocally distinguish between such an artificial brain and a real human being if we were unable to see, hear or touch either of them?

What sort of 'I-story' might a computer experience or be able to recount?[5]

Just what is the relationship between the mind and the body, between the 'I-story' and the 'brain-story'?

How can our material brains generate consciousness and self-awareness and make free choices, those free choices in turn influencing the material world?

To begin to answer questions of these kinds it would be helpful if we could define what we mean by 'consciousness' or by 'self-awareness'. Although, however, we all believe we possess these qualities and know in some sense what we mean by them, no one has yet come up with an adequate definition of what it means to be conscious. A great deal has been written about it, but a recent writer concludes, 'It does not seem to be possible to define consciousness in any meaningful way or to describe it in terms of other things.'[6] Nor has anyone come up with an adequate specification of the tests to be carried out to determine whether or not consciousness is possessed by a machine—or, for that matter, by an animal or a human being.

Not all that goes on in our brains is part of our conscious activity; most of the brain is concerned with the routine servicing of the various body's functions and with the processing of information. Recent research by neuro-physiologists and psychologists is beginning to indicate how some of the information is processed and what parts of the brain are involved in some parts of our conscious activity[7].

A strong correlation is found between activity in these parts of the brain and what we are conscious of doing. For instance, if we are concentrating on a particular scene, those parts of the brain which are responsible for the processing and interpretation of visual images are particularly active. Those same parts are also active if we think about a scene which is present in our memory, although we are not actually viewing it. Research also demonstrates that any particular conscious activity (such as viewing a scene) generally involves more than one part of the brain; the different parts of the brain which are participating are continually exchanging very large quantities of information[8]. This means that if one part of the brain is injured, the brain does not completely lose a particular function; it is in fact from the study of people with injured brains that much has been learnt about the functions of particular parts of the brain.

It is not just neuroscientists who are studying how physical processes in the brain are related to consciousness; physicists and mathematicians have also been tackling some of the fundamentals of the problem. Not that physics and mathematics provide the right expertise from which to tackle much of brain science; biology and biochemistry are mostly much more appropriate. But there are some basic problems concerned with the way we think and with the way the brain processes information which are a particular challenge to physicists. Roger Penrose[9] and Euan Squires[10] are two theoretical physicists who have considered in some detail how human consciousness and free will may be related to our present understanding of mathematics and physics.

Penrose begins by discussing in detail the fundamental character of the processes at the basis of mathematics and physics. I referred in the last chapter to his comments about the basic equations of physics that although they are deterministic they are not precisely computable, for fundamental mathematical reasons. The last chapter also explained that because 'chaos' is such a fundamental property of most natural systems, there are severe limits to our ability to predict their future behaviour. Although recognizing the important new perspective which an understanding of chaotic dynamics provides, Penrose does not believe that the non-computability of chaotic systems is adequate to move us very far forward with a basic understanding of the problems of human consciousness and free will. He comments that 'this is not the sort of non-computability that can be harnessed in any way' and 'if the brain is indeed calling upon useful non-computable elements in physical laws, they must be of a completely and much more positive character from this.'[11] Penrose therefore believes that, to make progress with an understanding of consciousness or free will, something much more fundamental needs to be injected than the realization of the extreme sensitivity of chaotic systems. He goes on to suggest what might be included in a way forward.

There is first the mathematical basis of the computing process itself. The fundamental logic governing the operation of all computers is based on the construction of algorithms (formal procedures for computation). But the development of mathematical methods goes far beyond the formal procedures required for computation. As is illustrated by Gödel's theorem (see box), the concept of

---

Gödel's theorem[12]

The formal methods of mathematics (as illustrated, for instance, by Euclid's geometry) depend on a set of basic assumptions or axioms from which other propositions or formal proofs can be developed. The aim of many mathematicians and logicians has been to develop a complete set of axioms and formal procedures by which everything in mathematics can be formally proved.

That aim was dealt a devastating blow in 1931 by a brilliant young Austrian mathematical logician, Kurt Gödel, who proved formally that any such system of axioms and procedures must contain some statements which are neither provable nor disprovable by the means available within the system. The development of mathematics, therefore, requires insights which are not contained within the mathematical system itself.

Penrose's CQG theory

In order to realize a mathematical and physical framework adequate to address the problem of human consciousness and free will, Roger Penrose[13] believes that a new theory is needed (he calls it correct quantum gravity: CQG). Such a theory must deal satisfactorily with some of the fundamental problems which currently exist and to which I have alluded in previous chapters. He considers in particular that the theory will:

● contain improved or replaced quantum mechanics

● incorporate gravity

● include time asymmetry in a natural way

● include aspects that are non-computable (and possibly non-deterministic).

The CQG theory will not just be a touching up of current physics; it will represent a major revolution. Penrose states, 'It is my opinion that our present picture of physical reality, particularly in relation to time, is due for a grand shake-up—even greater, perhaps, than that which has already been provided by present day relativity and quantum mechanics[14].

---

truth in mathematics is not just concerned with the truth of the formal axioms on which it is based. 'The concept of mathematical truth cannot be encapsulated in any formalistic scheme,' Penrose writes[15]. For mathematics to develop, the human mind and human consciousness must form judgments based on criteria independent of the mathematical system as to which algorithms make sense or are appropriate to a given problem. Penrose goes on to say:

I believe that our consciousness is a crucial ingredient in our comprehension of mathematical truth. We must 'see' the truth of a mathematical argument to be convinced of its validity. This 'seeing' is the very essence of consciousness. It must be present whenever we directly perceive mathematical truth. When we convince ourselves of the validity of Gödel's theorem we not only 'see' it but by so doing we reveal the very non-algorithmic nature of the 'seeing' process itself[16].

From the standpoint of mathematics, therefore, there appear to be fundamental arguments for believing that the brain is not just like a very complex electronic computer and that the computers we build, however large and complex they might become, cannot be expected to exhibit characteristics of consciousness. They cannot judge the applicability of the algorithms which program them to any given situation.

I now turn to the physics of the brain and ask whether there are any clues in our understanding of physics which might bear on our understanding of consciousness. Physics has developed enormously during this present century. Although there are some fundamental areas where progress is clearly required (for instance the detail of the processes which occurred in the Big Bang or the search for a theory of everything that unites gravity and quantum mechanics) most physicists feel that the sort of physics which applies to a structure of the scale and character of the brain is well-known. They find it hard to believe that discussion of the behaviour of the brain can be affected by the physics of the very fundamental processes which we have not yet elucidated.

Penrose does not agree. He concludes that 'we do not yet understand physics sufficiently well that the functioning of our brains can be adequately described in terms of it, even in principle'[17]. In support of this he first points out that the basic procedures of physics can all be expressed in terms of algorithms, whereas, as we have just seen, processes which cannot be contained within such formal procedures are associated with consciousness. Secondly, the basic equations of physics are symmetrical with respect to time (that is they can be applied equally well with time running backwards instead of forwards), whereas a perception of the flow of time is a basic ingredient of consciousness. Thirdly, the basic equations of physics are deterministic in character (the future as predicted by these equations is entirely determined by the past), whereas our common sense tells us that we all exercise free choices associated with our consciousness.

Penrose also believes that progress with the understanding of consciousness will come when radical new developments occur in our basic understanding of physics (see box). He concludes, 'It is our present lack of understanding of the fundamental laws of physics that prevents us from coming to grips with the concept of mind in physical or logical terms.'[18] Further, our understanding of determinism may well change after the grand shake-up, spoken of by Penrose, in our picture of physical reality has

---

Schrödinger's cat

In a box early in Chapter 6 I explained that because quantum theory is expressed through wave mechanics, the location and behaviour of elementary particles can never be completely defined. In Chapter 5 (the box on the Orsay Experiment), I described an experiment to test some of the results of quantum mechanics.

Consider a simple situation to which quantum mechanics can be applied, namely to an electron inside a metal approaching the metal's surface (which

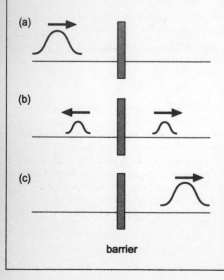

barrier

presents a barrier to the electron), where it may either be reflected back into the metal or transmitted so as to leave the solid surface. The hot wires emitting electrons in a television tube are practical examples of this situation.

Fig. 7.1 illustrates the quantum-mechanical description of the situation for a single electron. As it approaches the barrier it is described by a single wave function; afterwards the wave function is the sum of two parts: one associated with transmission, the other with reflection. Their relative sizes indicate the relative probabilities of reflection and transmission.

Suppose now that the electron has been observed to have been transmitted, for instance by observing a flash caused by it colliding with a fluorescent screen placed outside the metal surface. Then we know that there is no possibility of the electron

FIG. 7.1 (a) The quantum mechanical description, a wave function, of an electron approaching a barrier;
(b) the two parts of the wave function of the electron after it has left the barrier, one associated with reflection and the other with transmission and
(c) the 'collapsed' wave function describing the electron once it has been observed to have been transmitted.

occurred. New ideas about consciousness may bring new insights into determinism.

Squires, for his part, looks to the problem of interpretation which exists at the heart of quantum mechanics for a clue to the relation of consciousness to the physical

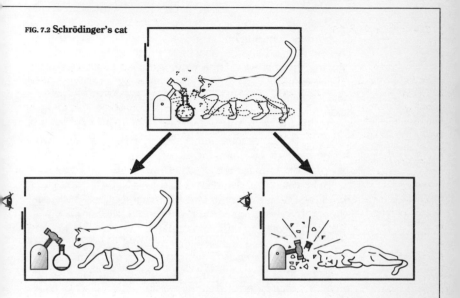

FIG. 7.2 Schrödinger's cat

having been reflected. The act of observation has caused the wave function to 'collapse' into the situation shown in Fig. 7.1(c).

To draw attention to the strangeness of the situation, Erwin Schrödinger, one of the pioneers of quantum mechanics, imagined the electron passing into an apparatus designed to operate a device which could poison a cat, all within the box containing

the experimental apparatus (Fig. 7.2). The quantum mechanical description will be a superposition of both a cat that is alive and one that is dead. Only when an observation is made as to whether the cat is alive or dead, by opening the box, will the description 'collapse' into one or the other[19].

world. In quantum mechanics a particle such as an electron is described by a wave function. In the standard interpretation of quantum mechanics, the wave function does not determine the electron's position; it only provides probabilities as to where it might be. If an observation of the position of an electron is made, its wave function will change to allow for the new knowledge provided by the observation (see box).

Squires homes in on the idea that it is the influence of the conscious mind of the observer which is responsible for causing the collapse of the wave function. This, of course, is not a new idea; it has been around ever since the development of quantum mechanics over fifty years ago and its implications have been widely debated. But Squires goes much further and speculates that in the relationship between the conscious mind and the part of the wave function which becomes the experienced reality there may be an opportunity for the exercise of free will[20]. It is not easy to see how such an idea relates to the actual processes going on in the brain, although, to a physicist, Squires' view that 'the problems of conscious mind and the problems of quantum theory are intimately related'[21] is a tantalizing one.

Whether or not Penrose's or Squires' speculations are correct, we are bound to conclude that there are fundamental problems in our current understanding of mathematics and physics which suggest that we cannot expect science as we know it now to account for the existence or operation of human consciousness or free will.

Biologists working on the science of the brain tend to be unimpressed with discussions like those of Penrose or Squires. The Nobel Prizewinner and neurobiologist, Gerald Edelman, describes physics, when applied to the mind, as the 'surrogate spook'[22]—in other words he considers it largely irrelevant to the mind-body problem. 'Until we reach a biological impasse,' he writes, 'we would do well to reject as a category error the notion that exotic physics itself will give a description of the observer's consciousness'[23]. Edelman believes that a theory of consciousness will come out of biology and psychology and describes ideas that might form the basis of the theory[24].

What seems clear from the discussion so far is that there are many areas of science which are relevant to any description of consciousness. These areas fall into many categories from the fundamental and logical (such as the mathematics and physics I have been describing) and the biological (such as the neuroscientific study of mechanisms in the brain) to the socio-psychological study of human behaviour. From no one of them (possibly not from any of them) will a complete scientific theory of human consciousness emerge. Much activity is taking place in all of them and we can expect a great deal of continuing debate as progress is made.

Is there a 'ghost' in the machine?

An assumption at the basis of nearly all the scientific activity I have been describing is that human consciousness and free will are characteristics which properly relate to the realm of physical description. Consciousness is not something which is added when all the material bits are in place; it is integral to our physical make-up. Human consciousness and free will form part of the 'scientific story' which is currently incomplete.

This assumption is very different from the traditional view that mind is something separate from matter, often referred to as the Cartesian view because of its association with the seventeenth-century philosopher and mathematician René Descartes. It is also known as dualism because of its distinction between the 'machine'—the matter of the brain, and the 'ghost in the machine'—the controlling conscious mind which is separate from the machine.

Philosophers and scientists have struggled with this problem ever since Descartes (and well before Descartes!) and, whether they would admit to it or not, many scientists still hold a basically dualistic view. Some have tried to identify the location of the 'ghost'. Descartes thought it might be located in the pineal gland; more recently others have looked in particular areas of the brain.

If the mind cannot be tied down to a particular location, can its operation be identified with a particular mechanism? I suppose that the motivation behind some of the explorations of fundamental physics to which I have given attention is one of hoping to pin down such a physical mechanism. But our conclusion that a theory of consciousness will involve many areas of science suggests that the operation of mind is unlikely to be found in any single mechanism (or even in several mechanisms).

As science has developed, concepts have sometimes been introduced that have later proved unnecessary and have been abandoned. Examples from physics are the caloric theory of heat and the theory that a substance called aether pervades all space (see box). The idea that the mind is something extra to the material in which its operation is apparent could also eventually prove to be superfluous.

Donald MacKay, a scientist who for many years studied the brain as a device for information processing, points out that 'there is an irreducible duality about our human nature—but this is a duality of aspects rather than of "substances"[25]. Further, when emphasising the importance of this holistic view, MacKay writes:

It would follow ... that there is no need—indeed it would be fallacious—to look for a causal mechanism by which mental and physical activity could act on one another. Their unity is already a closer (and a more mysterious) one than if they were pictured as separate activities in quasi-mechanical interaction, one of them visible and the other invisible.[26]

Other scientists have attempted to express this duality of aspects. Malcolm Jeeves, a professor of psychology, explains that 'mental activity is embodied in brain activity rather than being identical with brain activity[27]' and he quotes the psychologist and Nobel prizewinner Roger Sperry who concludes that 'consciousness is conceived to be a dynamic emergent property of brain activity, neither identical with nor reducible to, the neural events of which it is mainly composed'[28].

Thus, while rejecting any need to consider consciousness as an extra something added to the material which manifests it, we can also firmly reject reductionist views that might argue that consciousness is 'nothing but' any particular scientific description coming either from physics, biochemistry, biology or psychology. Each of these descriptions is addressing a particular part of the problem; they are complementary descriptions each with its own validity. Even if there were to emerge a new scientific description in some way integrated over a wide range of scientific disciplines, the same argument would apply; we could not say that consciousness was 'nothing but' the new scientific description. After all, there is the 'I-story', the expression of the conscious person, which is an equally valid (in some senses perhaps more valid) description of what consciousness is about. Although one of the objects of the scientific descriptions is to relate the 'brain story' to the 'I-story', the 'I-story' continues to have its own particular validity.

Some concepts in physics which have been abandoned

In the development of science, scientists have often battled with new concepts and how to fit them into the scientific structure of the time. Sometimes concepts have been introduced which have later proved to be unnecessary. One example is the caloric theory of heat which was introduced by Joseph Black, a Scottish chemist, in 1760. According to this theory, heat was thought to be some extra substance (called caloric) which was added to a hot object and taken away from a cold one. Eventually it was realized that heat was a due to the motions and vibrations of the atoms or molecules which make up the objects and therefore belonged to the objects themselves; there was no need for caloric.

Another example from physics is that of the aether, a substance which, it was postulated, filled all space and carried the means by which one body could exert gravitational pull on another, for instance by which the earth could attract the moon. Without the aether, such action at a distance seemed not to be possible. During the nineteenth century much effort was expended in looking for evidence of the existence of the aether, for instance the famous Michelson-Morley experiment which attempted to measure the movement of the earth relative to the aether. With the failure to find any evidence, eventually the idea of the aether was deemed unnecessary; action at a distance was accepted as due to different force fields, gravitational or electromagnetic, which did not require any substance to convey them.

It is the existence of the 'I-story' which introduces an entirely new and complicating feature into this discussion of the scientific approach to consciousness. If I am studying someone else's mind and brain I can, at least in principle, be objective about it. But if I attempt to study my own mind and brain it is impossible to carry out a full investigation or to be fully objective. I am the observer as well as the observed; any conclusions I may come to about the operation of my own brain and how it is related to my conscious thinking are bound to be limited and open to question.

The biologist J.B.S. Haldane expressed this point forty years ago when he wrote:

If my mental processes are determined wholly by the motions of the atoms in my brain, I have no reason to suppose that my beliefs are true ... and hence I have no reason for supposing my brain to be composed of atoms[29].

It may be that in the relationship between the mental and the physical levels of experience, there exists a fundamental limit to the degree of understanding which it is possible to achieve—a limit which is set by the fact that our own conscious activity is involved in that understanding. But I can also agree with John Polkinghorne when, after discussing this issue, he writes:

Until we know better how to integrate them [the mental and physical levels of experience] let us at least hold fast to our basic personal experience of choice and responsibility without denying the neurological insight that our mental activity is incarnated in our brains. These are complementary aspects of the whole person, just as wave and particle are complementary aspects of light[30].

Theological implications
We return now to consider what theological implications we can draw in the light of the scientific considerations I have addressed. How can they help us in the search for God and how God works in the world?

At the beginning of the chapter I drew a parallel between human consciousness and freedom of action and God's activity in the world. I now continue to pursue that parallel.

In the search for a scientific understanding of human consciousness and freedom of action I have outlined some of the suggestions which have been made regarding the relevance of chance and chaotic processes. Suggestions have also often been made that they provide flexibility through which God can be free to operate in the world. William Pollard[31], for instance, has suggested that God's influence in the world can be thought mainly to be at the sub-atomic level where there is real uncertainty (expressed formally in the uncertainty principle) inherent in the occurrence of events. This uncertainty, he believes, allows room for God's action while providing also for the maintenance of scientific consistency. Such a suggestion seems to restrict God to just tinkering in the margins or being limited to manoeuvres on a restricted scale—it is in fact another expression of the 'God of the gaps', even if this limited 'gap' were guaranteed to remain open.

John Polkinghorne has written extensively about the new perspective which arises from the realization that most processes going on in the world are complex, non-linear and therefore most probably chaotic. He sees large potential in the flexibility and openness of chaotic dynamics. 'The notion of flexible processes', he writes, 'helps us to see where there might be room for divine manoeuvre, within the limits of divine faithfulness.'[32] He goes on to say, 'The flexibility-within-regularity which chaotic dynamics suggests does appear appropriate to a world held in being by the God of love and faithfulness, whose twin gifts to his creation will be openness and reliability.'[33]

The insights of chaotic dynamics expressed in such statements certainly provide important new scientific and theological perspectives, very significantly different from those which pertained when the clockwork universe of Newtonian determinism was the dominant scientific model. As we have seen, the billions of bifurcations which are continually going on in our brains and in the world around us provide a framework for enormous flexibility, variety and novelty in the choices which are continually being made.

While I do not wish to underestimate the power of this new perspective, however, it clearly does not provide anything like the whole story either scientifically or theologically. Analysis earlier in the chapter has concluded that we are a very long way from any real scientific understanding of human consciousness and freedom of action. Before we will be able to match up the 'I-story' and the 'brain-story', enormous, perhaps revolutionary progress needs to be made in a wide range of sciences: mathematics, physics, biology, sociobiology and psychology. Even if such progress occurs, there remains the problem that it is our own consciousness, awareness and freedom which we are attempting to investigate— which may provide a fundamental limitation to the degree of understanding which it is actually possible to achieve.

When considering God's action in the world, our conclusions must be similar. It cannot be explained by or restricted to any particular mechanisms; we are not just looking for ways in which God might have room for manoeuvre. The whole of the 'scientific story' is God's story, together with the enormous consistency which it exhibits. Just as we saw that in attempting to match the 'I-story' and the 'brain-story' the whole range of scientific disciplines are involved, we can argue that in matching with the 'faith story', God has available to him the whole of the 'scientific story'. To understand God's activity in any lesser way would be inconsistent with the greatness and the character of God.

I have been at pains to point out that we cannot expect to understand God's action and its relation to the material universe until we have further insight into our own freedom of action and its connection to the material universe. At the heart of Christian belief is that we are made in the 'image of God'[34] and that our consciousness and free will are part of this image. As progress is made in understanding ourselves, therefore, we can anticipate also some development in theological insights regarding the way in which God works in the world.

There is also a part of the I-story which is particularly relevant to our interest here: the part which is related to experience of God. I talk, for instance, of having a relationship with God, of speaking with God in prayer, of being loved by God and loving him in return. These parts of the I-story are subjects for theological (and also psychological) investigation. They are also not something tacked on to the rest of the I-story and to be considered separate from it; they are as much, or more, part of me as any other part. Although it is often convenient to talk of various parts of our make-up (body, mind and spirit, for instance), science, philosophy and theology combine to emphasize the unity of each of us as a person. It is these connections with the spiritual world that I shall particularly be addressing in later chapters.

Let me conclude with a final point about God's activity. The message concluding Chapter 3 was that it was entirely reasonable to draw the inference that God is a personal, conscious Being, which leads on to the possibility of a relationship with him. In this chapter I have drawn a parallel between our freedom of action in the world and God's freedom. This implies that God is free to act, yet within his own constraints of order and regularity, as we are within ours.

There is a further limiting factor on God's actions. As the one also who has given human beings freedom—freedom to respond or reject, freedom to love or hate, freedom to do good or evil—God has limited himself to allow his creatures free will and true choice. I shall return to a consideration of these issues of freedom in Chapter 13 where we shall explore some of the implications for the way we pray.

However, first we must consider how we can describe this God and his possibility of relationship with us. Given that there is an inherent difficulty in describing the Creator of the universe in terms of created things, if we search for God there must be some way of knowing that our search has been successful.

Footnotes

1   This nomenclature was introduced by D.M. MacKay, *The open mind and other essays*, IVP, 1988, pp 104ff.

2   A parallelism discussed by A. Peacocke, 'God's action in the real world', *Zygon*, 26, 1991, pp 455–76.

3   See John Searle, *Minds, Brains and Science*, Penguin Books, 1984, Chapter 6, for discussion of this point.

4   A number of scientists and philosophers have argued this point. Donald MacKay (in *Brains, Machines and Persons*, Collins, 1980) has addressed formally the question of our freedom to choose, and has argued that because we are self-conscious beings, the reality of our freedom of choice is demanded on logical grounds—the choices we make cannot be logically determined. Euan Squires (in *Conscious Mind in the Physical World*, Adam Hilger, 1990, p 117) has pointed out that if a team of scientists wished to determine my future choice and action, the information they would need would imply the necessity for them to build an exact replica of my brain—exact in all respects. That an exact replica should take the same action as I do would not be surprising! Unless, of course, I came to know what it was predicted the replica would do—in which case I could always falsify it. These arguments have some appeal but I tend to agree with John Polkinghorne (in *One World*, SPCK, 1986, p 94) in being content with treating our freedom of choice as self-evident.

5   D.M. MacKay discusses these questions in *The open mind and other essays*, IVP, 1988, pp 102–137.

6   E. Squires, *Conscious Mind in the Physical World*, Adam Hilger, 1990, p 24.

7   John Horgan, in 'Can science explain consciousness?' *Sci. Amer.*, July 1994, pp 72–78, describes some of the burgeoning activity in this area of science.

8   Francis Crick, in *The Astonishing Hypothesis*, Simon and Schuster, 1994, describes what is known about the way the brain processes and interprets visual images.

9   *The Emperor's New Mind*, OUP, 1989 and *Shadows of the Mind*, OUP, 1994.

10   E. Squires, 1990, *op. cit.*.

11   R. Penrose, *The Emperor's New Mind*, p 225.

12   R. Penrose, *ibid*, pp 129 ff, also E. Squires *ibid* pp 146ff. For a very simplified proof of Gödel's theorem see R.D. Holder, *Nothing but atoms and molecules*, Monarch, 1993, pp 223–25.

13   R. Penrose, *ibid*, Chapters 8, 10.

14   R. Penrose, *ibid*, p 480.

15   R Penrose, *ibid*, p 145.

16   R. Penrose, *ibid*, p 540.

17   R. Penrose, *ibid*, p 194.

18   R. Penrose, *ibid*, p 4.

19   *The ghost in the atom*, ed. P.C.W. Davies & J.R. Brown, CUP, 1986, is a collection of interviews with prominent theoretical scientists about the mysteries of quantum physics.

20   E. Squires, 1990, *op. cit.*, p 213.

21   E. Squires, 1990, *op. cit.*, p 237.

22   Gerald Edelman, *Bright Air, Brilliant Fire, On the Matter of the Mind*, Penguin Books, 1992, p 212.

23   Gerald Edelman, *loc. cit.*, 1992, p 218.

24   Malcolm Jeeves, a professor of psychology, expounds the current status of brain science and the relation between mind and brain in *Mind Fields*, Lancer Books, Anzea Publishers, Australia, 1993 (also published under the Apollo imprint of IVP).

25   D.M. MacKay, *op. cit.*, 1988, p 56.

26   D.M. MacKay, 'Brain and will' in *Body and Mind*, ed. G.N.A. Vesey, George Allen and Unwin, 1964, pp 392–402.

27   M. Jeeves, *loc. cit.*, p 111.

28   M. Jeeves, *loc. cit.*, p 106.

29   J.B.S. Haldane, *Possible Worlds*, Chatto and Windus, London, 1945, p 209, quoted by M. Jeeves, *loc. cit:.*

30   J. Polkinghorne, *One World*, SPCK, 1986, p 96.

31   W.G. Pollard, *Chance and Providence*, Faber and Faber, 1959.

32   J. Polkinghorne, *Science and Providence*, SPCK, 1989, p 31.

33   J. Polkinghorne, 'A note on chaotic dynamics', *Science and Christian Belief*, **1**, 1989, pp 123–27.

34   Genesis 1:26–27

PART 3
How Can We Describe God?

L ooking for more data on God's sustaining presence in the universe, we must use our experience of the physical world in order to describe God who is not of that world—we have no other tools of description. Can taking a mathematical view of the universe as our guide help us in the search for God?

8 Space and Time

Nothing puzzles me more than time and space; and yet
nothing troubles me less, as I never think about them.
CHARLES LAMB

In thinking further about what we can learn about God
from the physical universe, it will help if we understand
something of the strong link between space and time
which underlies modern science. Scientists speak of
space-time, putting space and time together as one word;
they also speak of time as the fourth dimension. The
purpose of this chapter is to explain what is meant by
these expressions.

What do we mean by dimensions?

In Chapter 2, when describing events in the universe, I
noted that, because of the finite speed of light, we observe
far-off events not as they occur but at a certain time after
they have taken place, for instance the supernova
explosion in the Large Magellanic Cloud which was

FIG. 8.1 Diagrams in
two dimensions
(a) where any point
P has two
coordinates x and y
and in three
dimensions (b)
where any point P
has three
coordinates x, y
and z. Pythagoras'
theorem states that
the distance r from
the origin O to the
point P is given for
(a) by $r^2 = x^2 + y^2$
and for (b) by
$r^2 = x^2 + y^2 + z^2$.
The distance r does
not depend on the
choice of the
directions of the
axes of x, y and z.

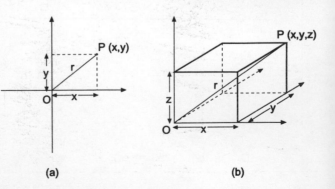

(a)　　　　　　　　　　　　　(b)

observed on 23 February 1987, some 155,000 years after it happened. An even more dramatic event was the supernova in the Crab Nebula which was observed on 4 July 1054 by Chinese astronomers, 5,000 years after its occurrence. Objects at the edge of the observable universe are seen now as they were perhaps 10 thousand million years ago. In this description of the universe, space and time are inextricably linked.

We speak of the 'dimensions' of space and time. What do we mean by these? The three dimensions of space at right

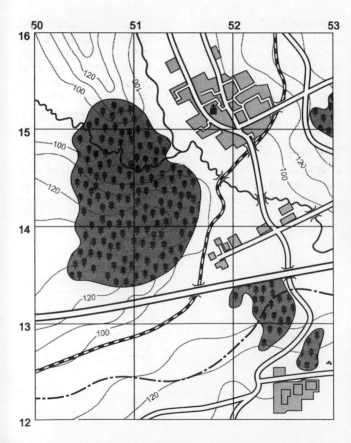

FIG. 8.2 Any position on an Ordnance Survey map can be described by three numbers—two being the coordinates in the British National Grid Reference System, the third being the height above sea level. Because the Grid Reference System is a flat, square grid—large squares are 100km on a side—superimposed on the spherical surface of the Earth, the sides of any square in the grid are not precisely N-S or E-W. A key on each map explains how far 'grid north' is from 'true north'. The information provided can also relate the grid reference to latitude and longitude. The choice of grid pattern or its orientation makes no difference to the distances between locations on the map.

angles to each other (Fig. 8.1) are familiar enough to us, often conveniently described as the directions (or axes, when displayed on a graph) of north-south, east-west and up-down, or as the measurements of length, width and height (Fig. 8.2). But they do not have to be defined in that way.

For instance, if I make a plan of my house, it is convenient to choose the directions of the two horizontal axes of the plan to be along the front of the house and along its side. But I could, if I chose, make other selections. The choice of axes makes no difference to the shape of the rooms or the width of the doors, but is made purely for ease of representation on the plan. The third dimension can be represented by drawing elevations of various parts of the structure of the house. For these it is normally convenient to choose the horizontal as one dimension and the vertical as the other. However, in drawing the roof structure, other axes may be selected to bring out particular features of the

FIG. 8.3 A distance-time plot of trains travelling between Oxford (O), Reading (R) and London (L) between 0900 and 1500 on weekdays.

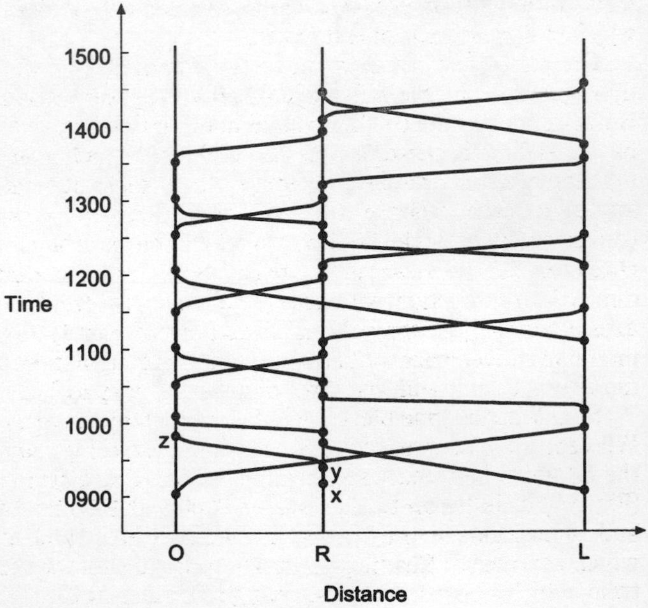

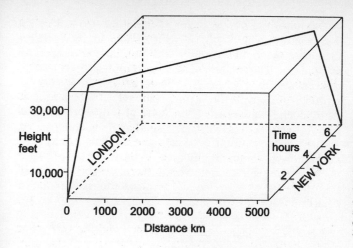

FIG. 8.4 A distance-height-time plot of an aircraft flight from London to New York, 5500km and 7 hours' flying time away. Much of the flight is spent at the cruising altitude of 35,000 ft.

construction. If the drawings have been done correctly, the same answer will be obtained for any particular measurement within the house, whatever the axes chosen from which that measurement is deduced.

On Earth it is usual to draw plans in the horizontal dimensions, and elevations including a vertical dimension. However, out in space, 'horizontal' and 'vertical' cease to have meaning, because there is no fixed point of reference. For engineering drawings in space, three axes at right angles to each other would still be chosen, to be as convenient as possible, but this would still be an arbitrary choice. In the universe as a whole there is no preferred dimension or direction; we define the directions of the three axes describing our three-dimensional universe purely as a matter of convenience. But how can time be brought in as a dimension to link with the three dimensions of space?

Simple space-time plots are in fact quite familiar to us. We can, for instance, plot train journeys covering, say, the 63 miles between Oxford and London. The diagram (Fig. 8.3) includes all times between 0900 and 1500 hours and all positions on the railway line. Point X is the time at which I arrived at Reading Station in order to wait for the train, which I boarded at Y, arriving at Oxford at Z.

Having drawn a diagram of one dimension of space with one of time, it is not difficult to imagine a three-dimensional model having two dimensions of space and one of time. The model could, for example, use as spatial dimensions the horizontal position and the vertical altitude of aircraft flying in a direct line between, say, London and New York (Fig. 8.4). The third dimension could be marked off in hours so that lines constructed within the model could be used to read off the position of aircraft on that route at any given time after take-off. Any point within the model would be described by three coordinates: two of space, say y (horizontal position) and z (altitude) and one of time, t.

Space-time geometry[1]

In the ordinary geometry of space, a point signifies an object located at specific coordinates x, y, z from a given origin O where the axes meet (Fig. 8.1). In space-time geometry a point signifies an event—an object at a certain point in time. Fig. 8.5 is a space-time diagram with one space dimension x, and a time dimension t. The observer is at a particular point O at the present time. Events in the past are in the lower half of the diagram and those in the future in the upper half.

The scales of the two axes can be arranged so that light signals travel along lines at 45° to the axes. For instance, since the velocity of light is 300,000 km/s, if along the time axis 1 cm represents 1 second, then along the space axis 1 cm would represent 300,000 km. From the past, light signals arriving at O travel along PO and QO; they can continue into the future along OR and OS. Since no information can travel faster than light, the observer at O can only

be aware of events in the past within the shaded area of the diagram; an event at N, for instance, cannot communicate with O. Similarly the observer at O can only have influence on events in the future within the shaded area.

By analogy with distances in three-dimensional space, which are independent of the choice of axes, 'distances' between events in the four-dimensional model can also be defined. In Minkowski space-time geometry, events are linked by light signals such that the 'distance' r of an event from the origin O is given by $r^2 = x^2 - c^2 t^2$ (if we include three space dimensions x, y, z, it is $r^2 = x^2 + y^2 + z^2 - c^2 t^2$).

The presence of the minus sign before the term containing time occurs because in Minkowski geometry, time is plotted in units of ic where c is the velocity of light and i is the square root of -1. Mathematicians call quantities multiplied by i 'imaginary' quantities (see glossary); the 'complex'

Following on from this, it is now perhaps not too difficult to imagine a four-dimensional model in which points are described by three space coordinates x, y and z, and one time coordinate t. Although we cannot, of course, actually construct such a model, we can write down the rules for its geometry, and calculate the quantities involved using these rules.

Time as the fourth dimension

In the models I have mentioned so far, time and space are distinct. A big leap in thought was made by the Russian physicist Minkowski in 1908, when he put space and time together in a geometrical model in such a way that some of

geometry which results from dealing with such quantities has many applications—although in popular jargon an element of mystery seems to have been introduced into this fourth dimension with its 'imaginary' character. 'Imaginary time' was also mentioned in Chapter 4, in the context of Hawking's theory of the universe's beginning.

A further result of the presence of the minus sign in the Minkowski geometry expression for 'distance' is that these 'distances' between events cannot be represented by lengths on a diagram. Note, for instance, that in Fig. 8.5 the value of r is zero along the diagonal lines taken by light signals connecting with O; along these lines $x = ct$ or $x = -ct$. The rules for Minkowski geometry can be written down, but it cannot satisfactorily be drawn on paper.

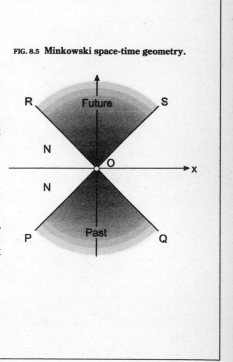

FIG. 8.5 **Minkowski space-time geometry.**

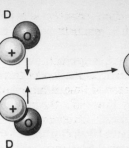

FIG. 8.6 The shining of the sun is our nearest extraterrestrial example of mass-to-energy conversion. When two nuclei of deuterium D (heavy hydrogen) fuse to form a helium (He) nucleus, mass m is lost and energy E released in the process, which is the sun's source of energy. According to the formula $E = mc^2$, which is a result of Einstein's theory of relativity, every gramme of lost mass releases 30 million kWh of energy.

FIG. 8.7 Where is the edge of the universe?

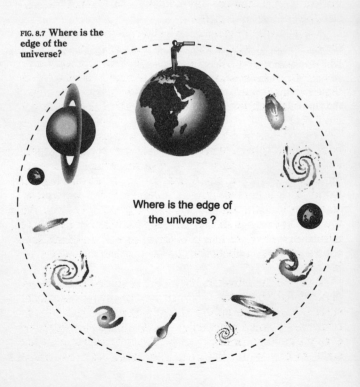

Where is the edge of the universe ?

118

the distinction between space and time is removed. In Minkowski's geometry, time is made to look like space (Fig. 8.5).

Minkowski's geometrical model of space-time (see box) was such that in the model there is no preferred direction and no preferred time. It turned out to be an effective way of describing Einstein's theory of relativity. In this theory, Einstein in 1905 elaborated the simple principles that there is no preferred velocity and that there can be no velocity greater than the velocity of light in a vacuum, c. These principles, which are rather simply embodied in the Minkowski geometry, led to many results fundamental to modern physics. The most important and well-known of these is the equivalence of mass and energy; mass can be destroyed and energy released (Fig. 8.6). Atomic bombs and nuclear power stations are familiar earthbound demonstrations of this equivalence.

The success of the model, which gives space-time a four-dimensional structure, has led cosmologists to think of geometrical models of the universe. The most widely publicized of these is one in which the universe is a three-dimensional 'spherical' surface embedded in the four-dimensional space-time continuum. That sounds rather a mouthful!

A good idea of what is meant can be acquired by going back to the three-dimensional world we understand and looking at the surface of the Earth, which is a two-dimensional surface embedded in the three-dimensional world. It is a curved surface, although when we look at small parts of the Earth such as our garden, or even the town we live in, it is so close to being flat that for all normal purposes we neglect its curvature. Because the Earth is a sphere it is an unbounded surface; it has no edges, no boundaries.

Being in the universe, the model suggests, is the three-dimensional equivalent of being on the two-dimensional surface of a large sphere. Locally (and by 'locally' the cosmologist would mean on the scale of the solar system or even the galaxy), for nearly all purposes the curvature is too small to be noticed. But on a very large scale the whole

FIG. 8.8 Expansion of the surface of a balloon which is being inflated is like the expansion of the universe. No matter which part of the pattern on the balloon is marked with an X, all the other parts of the pattern move away from it, the pieces furthest from the X moving the fastest.

universe is curved in such a way that if we travelled in a straight line far enough and fast enough we would arrive back at our starting-point (Fig. 8.7). I say 'fast enough' because, as we saw in Chapter 2, the universe is expanding and we would have to travel impossibly fast to beat the expansion.

On the same model, the expansion of the universe is compared with the 'spherical' surface which expands when a balloon is blown up (Fig. 8.8). It begins at a very small size, then all parts of the surface expand uniformly; letters on the balloon, small and almost unreadable to begin with, become larger and larger, but all in proportion, as the balloon expands.

An important part of the conception of this model is that it is the space-time continuum which is expanding with the material and radiation within it. It is not that the material and radiation is expanding into empty regions of space-time; after all, there are no boundaries or edges to space-time over which the expansion can occur!

Whether the universe will continue expanding, or reach a limit and then contract; whether in fact the space-time continuum of the universe is spherical or some more complex shape, are matters still hotly in debate among cosmologists. Whatever their conclusions, linking space and time in this way has produced a revolution in our way of understanding the physical world, both on the atomic and the cosmological scales.

Footnotes

1   More extended semi-popular expositions of space-time geometry can be found in *Space and Time in the Modern Universe* by P.C.W. Davies, CUP, 1977 and *Extra-Galactic Adventure* by J. Heidmann, CUP, 1982.

9 A Fifth Dimension

Plato said that God geometrizes continually.
PLUTARCH

In the last chapter we saw how much new understanding of the physical world flowed from the development of a geometrical model of the universe possessing four dimensions, three of space and one of time. We saw that not only is such a model helpful in aiding understanding but it is also an essential tool in predicting the behaviour of physical systems, such as the expansion of the universe. In this chapter I suggest that a similar model can provide an analogy which can help us think about God's presence in the world.

Models

Scientists are continually inventing models to help in their descriptions. For instance, the nucleus of an atom is extremely small, less than one millionth millionth (10^{-12}) of a centimetre in diameter, yet it contains many particles held together by a variety of forces. To assist in understanding the structure of the atomic nucleus, scientists talk of the shell model (in which the particles are imagined to be arranged in concentric shells, as electrons are arranged in atoms) or of the liquid-drop model (in which the forces between particles are imagined to be similar to the forces between molecules in a drop of liquid). In a completely different field, scientists investigating the operation of the brain build models of aspects of its behaviour, relating them to the basic functions of a computer. Again, meteorologists build computer models of the atmospheric circulation for forecasting the future weather. Models of all kinds— thought models, computer models, scale models, practical models—are fundamental tools in scientific investigation.

Models are also part of the stock-in-trade of the theologian. Religious language constantly employs analogies or models. For instance, Jesus in his parables introduced 'models' of the kingdom of heaven. The kingdom of heaven is like a man sowing seed, like a woman baking bread, like a grain of mustard seed, like treasure hidden in a field, like a merchant in search of fine pearls, like a net gathering fish, and so on[1]. Parables, metaphors, analogies and models abound in the New Testament and in the parlance of the modern preacher.

So I believe it is in the best possible tradition for us to pursue scientific models to help us in expressing religious ideas. We have, for instance, great difficulty in knowing how to talk about where to find God. As a child I was taught that he is 'above the bright blue sky'. As an adult, especially as an adult scientist, I find that model unsatisfactory. Can science help by providing something better?

A scientific analogy

The crucial step in the space-time model described in the last chapter was the introduction of time as the fourth dimension. I want here to introduce a scientific analogy or model which I have found very useful in thinking about the way God works in the world.

I want to suggest that we can think about God's relation to the universe as if he were present in an extra dimension as well as in those in which we live. To add such a further dimension is to add something very substantial to our idea of God. Just as three-dimensional objects are solid compared with two-dimensional ones, the model we have developed suggests that heaven—defined as where God is—with its extra spiritual dimension is a place of greater 'solidity' than the material world we know.

C.S. Lewis pursues a similar analogy in his book *The Great Divorce*[2], in which he pictures inhabitants of hell arriving at the outskirts of heaven. Compared with the solid people from heaven who go to meet them, they appear as shadowy phantoms, transparent to the brightness of the place, pained by the roughness and sharpness of the solid objects around them, even of the blades of grass on which they walk.

However, thinking in more than three dimensions is difficult for most people. Let us begin by trying to imagine life in a two-dimensional world. In a fascinating book called *Flatland*, written just over one hundred years ago in the 1880s, a mathematician, Edwin Abbott, imagines such a world (Fig. 9.1). The inhabitants of this world are confined to move on a horizontal plane surface, and indeed have no knowledge whatever of anything outside that plane. They

FIG. 9.1 The cover of Abbott's book *Flatland*.

experience north-south and east-west but cannot begin to conceive of up-down. For them the third dimension does not exist.

The inhabitants of Abbott's two-dimensional world are beings whose outlines are mathematical figures: straight lines, triangles, squares, pentagons and so on, up to circles. A being's class in Flatland society is determined by the number of sides possessed. The lowest class are the needle-shaped straight lines; they are the women of Flatland—remember the book was written a hundred years ago! The highest class are the circles, with an infinite number of sides; they are the priests of Flatland. Abbott describes in detail how the different classes recognize each other and keep out of each other's way; the book was, in fact, written as a satire on class.

Towards the end of Abbott's book, a sphere from the three-dimensional world of Spaceland appears, and attempts to explain to one of the two-dimensional beings of Flatland what it means to possess another dimension and be a sphere. In order to demonstrate its nature, the sphere passes vertically through the horizontal plane of Flatland several times (Fig. 9.2), appearing first as a point, followed by a small circle, a larger circle, then a smaller circle again before it disappears—a process completely inexplicable and magical to the Flatland inhabitants. The sphere then demonstrates that by moving above the Flatland plane it can see into the interior of Flatland houses, rooms and cupboards and even into the innards of the Flatland beings themselves, without

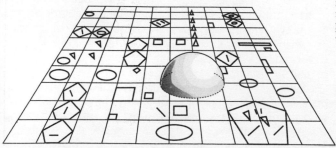

FIG. 9.2 A sphere from Spaceland passing through Flatland.

passing through the doors and windows—again, a capacity utterly mysterious to the Flatlanders.

Finally, the incredulous Flatlander is taken out of Flatland by the sphere from Spaceland and given a vision of the three-dimensional world. However, on returning to Flatland he is completely unable, either through his attempts at description or through mathematical analogy, to persuade his fellow Flatlanders to give any credence to his new-fangled ideas. To them everything in Flatland is complete; there is nothing they perceive in their everyday life which cannot be described in two-dimensional terms. His seeing the circle and then not seeing the circle, and his conversation with this illusory being, were clearly hallucinations; things like that just did not happen in Flatland. To imagine any other than a two-dimensional framework for their existence seemed impossible and unnecessary.

We suffer from the same problem as the Flatlanders, and often have great difficulty imagining anything outside our material four-dimensional world of space and time. But, by way of analogy, let us imagine God to be in another dimension—let us call it the spiritual dimension—additional to the four-dimensional world of space and time which we can see, touch and handle. Can this analogy help us in thinking about God and his relationship to the universe?

We recall that the sphere outside Flatland is aware of all parts of Flatland; all events in Flatland are transparent to it. Further, it can enter and be present in Flatland anywhere it pleases. In a similar way, we can imagine God in the spiritual dimension being 'outside' the bounds of our material universe, yet all-seeing and all-knowing regarding events within it, and having the ability to be present anywhere within it. In theological terms, God is both transcendent, that is, apart from the universe, and immanent, that is, present within the universe.

This analogy is helpful in our thinking about the question 'Where is God?' But why have I called the spiritual dimension not the fourth but the fifth? I have done this deliberately because the analogy is also helpful in aiding our understanding of God's relation to time.

Time is an integral component of the material universe. Its observation and measurement are intimately linked with material events: the movement of sand through the hourglass, the swinging of a pendulum, the beating of a heart, the rotation of the Earth. It has meaning to us only in this physical context, and we have seen in Chapter 8 how the dimensions of space and time link together in the creation of models of the structure of the universe.

Considering time as a dimension with similar characteristics to a dimension of space—as modern physics encourages us to do—enables us to think of God as outside time as well as outside space. Using this analogy, he can also enter the space-time world and appear within time. In our theological terminology, God is transcendent and immanent with respect to both space and time. In other words, he is both in some sense outside time and also in a real sense present within the time of our universe.

In our material existence we are so much creatures of time that the idea of being outside time seems an even more difficult concept than being outside space. A very different analogy or model which may be helpful in this respect is due to the writer Dorothy L. Sayers, who imagines God as the author of the human drama.

To the audience watching a play on the stage, the plot unfolds gradually; all may be mysterious until the very last moment before the final curtain falls. Though the years covered by the drama are compressed to an hour or two in the theatre, the characters who take their place in the story come with a ready-made history. They have no knowledge of events in their future. The playwright, however—the creator of the drama—has conceived the whole plot from beginning to end. He or she knows the whole story, the order of events within the play and how the final scene will emerge. Thus the author can be said to be 'outside' the time of the drama. However, there is also the possibility of the playwright becoming one of the players and thus entering in some sense into the time-frame of the drama.

This model, like all models, has its limitations. We are all seen as players on the stage, reading a prepared script. The author of the drama could perhaps allow some freedom to the players, but the model would still not do justice to human freedom and responsibility. However, it remains helpful in stretching our thinking about the dimension of time. I shall return later in this chapter to address further the problems involved in thinking about God both within and outside time.

A further point can be made regarding the way dimensions interact with each other. A structure of two dimensions is completely contained within a world of three dimensions. Our model therefore suggests that the structure of heaven with its five dimensions contains the four dimensions which make up the material world; under this analogy, the space and time dimensions we know are part of the fabric of heaven. Rather than speaking of God and heaven as being outside space and time, it might be better to speak of them transcending space and time.

In other words, although space and time are part of the structure of heaven, many of the limitations and constraints which they impose on events and movements in the four-dimensional space-time world are removed by the addition of a further dimension. Not only is there greater solidity in heaven, there is greater freedom.

Limitations of analogy

In this chapter, I have been presenting models to assist us in thinking about God and where God is. But we need to realize they are, of course, only analogies which help us to think about reality; they are not reality itself, and are bound to be extremely limited in their representation of that reality. As with all analogies they must not be overplayed; especially must this be the case when we are attempting to describe God.

Hilary of Poitiers, a fourth-century Christian, puts the point well 'There can be no comparison between God and earthly things,' he writes, 'but the weakness of our understanding forces us to seek certain images from a lower level to serve as pointers to things of a higher level. Hence every comparison is to be regarded as helpful to men rather than suited to God since it suggests rather than exhausts the meaning we seek.'[3]

Some might question whether it is not improper or irreverent to think about God using such analogies. Are we trying to confine God by finding a slot for him and calling it the fifth dimension? Such a danger is always there, although that is not, of course, my intention. On the contrary, what I have done is to look for analogies and models which do not confine God but which stretch our thought and imagination to think of him in ways which enhance his greatness.

These ideas are not new

We should also realize that although the vocabulary used in the fifth-dimension analogy is familiar to people with a modern scientific education, the ideas themselves are not new. In fact, they are present explicitly or implicitly in Hebrew and Christian thought from the earliest times.

Many of the Jews and early Christians thought in somewhat spatial terms and imagined heaven, the dwelling-place of God, to be within a celestial sphere surrounding the Earth. They clearly found that a helpful picture. However, as expressed in the biblical writings, they did not try to confine God to a particular location. He was thought of as a spiritual being both outside the universe he had created and also present within it. God's transcendence and immanence pervade the whole of the Bible. Let us look at a few examples.

☐ Moses, when confronted by a burning bush which is not consumed[4],realizes that God is not only in heaven but also present there within the bush. The name I AM by which God is called in that story gives hints too, of his timelessness through his being ever present.

☐ Solomon, in his prayer of dedication for the elaborate temple he had built in Jerusalem, exclaims: 'But will God really dwell on the Earth? The heavens, even the highest heaven, cannot contain you. How much less this temple I have built! Yet give attention to your servant's prayer and his plea for mercy, O Lord my God.'[5] The concept of God's transcendence is put

129

alongside the belief that God hears prayer and is active in the world.

☐ Of all the prophets—people who spoke out on behalf of God—Isaiah is probably the one with the clearest view of God as creator and sustainer of the universe. God 'sits ... above the circle of the Earth ... stretches out the heavens like a canopy, and spreads them out like a tent to live in.'[6] He created the stars, bringing out 'the starry host one by one'.[7] God 'inhabiteth eternity'; he dwells 'in the high and holy place, with him also that is of a contrite and humble spirit.'[8] Thus Isaiah juxtaposes God's transcendence and his immanence.

☐ As a final example, moving to the period of the early church, we find the apostle Paul standing on Mars Hill, preaching to the Athenians and making use of ideas of the immanence of God present in contemporary Greek writings. He tells them that 'God who made the world and everything in it ... does not live in temples built by hands ... he is not far from each one of us. "For in him we live and move and have our being."'[9].

God and time

Because it raises real difficulties of thought, I return now to explore further the concept of God both within and outside time.

Time is so much part of the framework in which we operate that it is virtually impossible to imagine any operation which excludes it. Although scientific thinking since Einstein has recognized that time is relative, in the sense that it can be different for different observers, none of that has removed the vital difference between 'before' and 'after' in any given framework or the reality of cause preceding effect.

Theologians and philosophers have for centuries struggled with the problem of how God is related to time[10]. In their discussions they have differentiated between God outside time and God within time. Our model of the spiritual dimension illustrates God in both of these.

Let us first look at God's immanence with respect to time—that is, God within time. Christians believe that God entered time supremely in the person of Jesus. As a human being Jesus, before his resurrection, was clearly subject to the limitations of space and time. Although he possessed remarkable insights and there are hints that on occasions, he had a clear view of future events—his own death[11], for instance, and Peter's denial of knowing him[12]—there are other occasions when he either expressed ignorance of the future[13] or prayed for it to be changed. 'May this cup pass from me,' he asked in Gethsemane under the stress of impending crucifixion[14].

But it is not only in God incarnate in Jesus that we meet God within time. Although the Hebrew writers of the Old Testament thought of God as eternal and timeless[15], they also saw him as closely involved with their day-to-day existence. He could show favour or be displeased[16], he could change his mind in response to human behaviour or request[17]—all characteristics of someone present and active within time. It has been pointed out, for instance by Paul Fiddes[18], that in order for God to share in human experiences and to experience suffering in the way that both the Old Testament and the New Testament affirm[19], it is necessary for God to experience time in a sequential way ('before' and 'after') with the possibility of change which that implies. The experience of God within time, alongside human beings is one that is central to the Christian faith.

But it does not do justice to the biblical view of God or to the tradition and experience of Christians to speak only of God within time. As our model suggests, God is also outside time just as he is also outside our framework of space. Being outside time is more difficult to imagine than being outside space. What do we mean by it?

It is, I think, being able to see something all at once. We can perhaps get some idea of it by thinking about the way we view a beautiful landscape or a fine picture. We may look for some time at some of the parts that make up the landscape or the picture, but to really appreciate it we need to view it as a whole. The passage of time is not involved in such viewing except in so far as we know we cannot hold on to it; reluctantly we have to move on.

Perhaps the nearest we can come to experiencing timelessness is in those comparatively rare flashes of inspiration when, for instance, the solution to a complex problem we have been thinking about for weeks comes to us in a moment. Although, not apparently going through the sequence of argument, we feel convinced in that moment that we have hit on the solution.

Roger Penrose[20] cites some examples of such moments of inspiration experienced by mathematicians, pointing out that it is often the apparently aesthetic character of the solution, its beauty or its elegance which provides the inspirational appeal of the solution-in-a-flash. Artists can experience similar inspiration. A striking example is provided by Mozart's apparent ability to experience and appreciate, at the moment of composition, a lengthy piece of music all at once. 'My mind seizes it as a glance of my eye a beautiful picture or a handsome youth,' he wrote. 'It does not come to me successively, with various parts worked out in detail, as they will later on, but it is in its entirety that my imagination lets me hear it[21].'

To picture God outside time is not to imagine him as static or uninvolved but as seeing creation—its complete span of space and time—as a whole. The purpose-making, the planning, the unfolding of the drama with all its interconnected parts, combine to make up that whole.

We may find it just about possible to conceive God within time and even of God outside time, but thinking of God as both together really is difficult. John Polkinghorne[22] talks of God 'being' (God outside time) and God 'becoming' (God within time) as the two opposite poles of the model, and Donald MacKay[23] distinguishes between two persons in one Godhead: God-in-eternity and God-in-time; God transcendent and God immanent.

Despite its technical language, this model is not new. It is reflected in words which I have already quoted earlier in the chapter, spoken well before the Christian era by the prophet Isaiah who presented God as 'inhabiting eternity' but also dwelling 'with him that is of a contrite and humble spirit'[24].

Not surprisingly, however, that is not the only problem we have in thinking about God! Another question, just as old, concerns how God can be ruling the universe in heaven, yet simultaneously present in the person of Jesus, and also working in the world through his Spirit. This problem concerning God's immanence and transcendence with respect to space is similar to the problem with respect to time which I have just described. To assist in overcoming it, the doctrine of the Trinity has been developed—God manifest in three persons, Father, Son and Holy Spirit. In scientific language, the Trinity is a model of God which helps us to think about his relation to space, and again, it is not a new idea—Paul used it in one of his letters to the church at Corinth[25].

In this chapter I have suggested that, through the analogy of the fifth dimension, it is possible to think of God as transcending and yet within both space and time. The question may be asked, however, whether there is any point in attempting to stretch our thinking by these analogies. Are they just of academic interest, or are they of help, for instance, in getting to know God? I will argue in later chapters that although we are creatures limited by the four dimensions of space and time it is possible to have knowledge of God in the spiritual dimension, knowledge which is also relevant to our material existence.

Footnotes

1 These parables can be found in the Gospel of Matthew, Chapter 13.

2 Fontana, 1972.

3 Quoted by T.F. Torrance in *Space, Time and Incarnation*, OUP, 1969.

4 Exodus 3.

5 1 Kings 8:27–28.

6 Isaiah 40:22.

7 Isaiah 40:26.

8 Isaiah 57:15 (Authorized Version).

9 Acts 17:24, 27–28.

10 See, for instance, N.Pike, *God and timelessness*, Routledge and Kegan Paul, 1970, and W.S. Anglin, *Free will and the Christian faith*, Clarendon Press, 1990.

11   Matthew 20:18, 19; Mark 8:31, 10:33.

12   Mark 14:30, 72.

13   With respect to his own future return: Matthew 24:36.

14   Matthew 26:39.

15   For example Psalm 90:1–4.

16   For example Genesis 6:6–8, 1 Samuel 15:10.

17   For example Jeremiah 18:8, Jonah 3:10, Hosea 11:8.

18   *The creative suffering of God*, Clarendon Press, 1988 pp 91–100.

19   For example Genesis 6:6, Hosea 11:8, Hebrews 2:18, 4:15.

20   R. Penrose, *The Emperor's New Mind*, OUP, 1989, pp 541–47.

21   Quoted by R. Penrose, *loc. cit.*, p 547.

22   J. Polkinghorne, *Science and Providence*, SPCK, 1989, Chapter 7.

23   D.M. MacKay, *The open mind and other essays*, IVP, 1988, p 193.

24   Isaiah 57:15 (Authorised Version)

25   2 Corinthians 13:14.

PART 4
The Nature
of God

We have explored the nature of the universe, God's role in both creating and sustaining it and his presence in the 'spiritual dimension'. However, we are no nearer finding out what God is really like, other than a supposition that the Designer of human beings must also have personal qualities. A person can only really be known by self-revelation, however much external data we may have collected about that person. Has God revealed himself in this way?

10 A Personal God

The Son is the radiance of God's glory and the exact representation of his being.
HEBREWS 1:3

In Chapter 4, in introducing the concept of the 'faith story' as well as the 'scientific story', I pointed out that the 'faith story' presupposes a personal relationship with God— that is what faith is about. Although we may often feel more comfortable with a remote, relatively undemanding God, one who is behind the 'scientific story' perhaps but not otherwise accessible, we also feel the strong urge to search for more knowledge of God and for closer contact. In this chapter I want to explore the nature of that closer relationship, presented in the context of the Christian faith.

Some limited knowledge of other people can be gained from knowing about what they have done. But we can really get to know another person only if that person communicates with us, through the variety of means of expression with which we as human beings are familiar. It follows that we can find out about God's personality only if he chooses to communicate with us. At the centre of the Christian faith is the belief that God has done just that, not in a way outside our normal experience—like the futile attempt of the sphere from Spaceland to communicate with the inhabitants of Flatland—but in the person of a unique human being, Jesus. It is hard to think of any other way in which communication of God's personal character could be arranged; personality can be conveyed only through personality. Even so, the incarnation, the technical term theologians use for the coming of God into our human world, not surprisingly raises profound difficulties of comprehension—a problem to which I shall return in the next chapter.

Metaphors which describe Jesus

The best way to begin to appreciate the character and personality of Jesus is to sit down with as fresh a mind as possible, and read, preferably in a modern translation, the accounts we have of his life, death and resurrection— rising from death—as presented by the four Gospel writers. Since my interest here, however, is in exploring helpful analogies which can assist in our search for connections between ourselves, the universe and God, it is worth looking briefly at some of the metaphors used by the New Testament writers and by Jesus himself to illustrate his character and his role in acting as a bridge between humanity and God.

The fourth Gospel, the Gospel of John, begins with a telling metaphor: that Jesus is the Word of God. It would immediately have struck chords with readers from both Jewish and Greek backgrounds[1]. To the Jew the word of the Lord was an extension of the divine personality, invested with the divine authority; for instance, 'By the word of the Lord were the heavens made.'[2] To the Greek, the Word (the Greek word *Logos*) represents God's self-expression and includes the idea of the rational principle behind the universe. By introducing such a metaphor right at the start of his Gospel, John establishes common ground with readers coming from widely different backgrounds.

Also in John's Gospel, Jesus unequivocally identifies himself with God, whom he calls Father: 'Anyone who has seen me has seen the Father,'[3] replies Jesus to a question from one of his disciples about how they can see God, 'the Father'. The name 'I AM', which was one of the Jewish names for God (see Chapter 9), was also taken to himself by Jesus. The religious leaders were puzzled that Jesus could claim personal knowledge of Abraham, who had lived so many centuries before. 'You have seen Abraham!' they jibed—to which Jesus replied, 'Before Abraham was born, I am.' The religious leaders took this remark with its use of the divine name 'I AM' as a claim to deity, and took up stones to try to kill him as a blasphemer[4].

Further in the same Gospel, seven down-to-Earth metaphors are introduced, through which Jesus tells people about himself:

☐ 'I am the bread of life.' (6:35)

☐ 'I am the light of the world.' (9:5)

☐ 'I am the gate for the sheep.' (10:7)

☐ 'I am the good shepherd.' (10:11)

☐ 'I am the resurrection and the life.' (11.25)

☐ 'I am the way and the truth and the life.' (14:6)

☐ 'I am the true vine.' (15:1)

All of them emphasize the basic human need for a relationship with God. And they emphasize the reality of a life as real as, but more fundamental and more lasting than, our physical life. Variously called spiritual life or eternal life, it is not something other-worldly that has no connection with our physical existence and everyday experience. Rather, the point Jesus is constantly illustrating by his words and by his life is that only if proper connections are made to the spiritual dimension can life on Earth with its ambitions and relationships be properly fulfilled.

The first and the last metaphors emphasize the truth that 'man does not live on bread alone'[5]. Just as there is a need to nourish physical life, so spiritual life too needs sustaining. The striking claim made by Jesus is that he is the source of this sustenance. We need to feed on the bread of life and to draw strength from the true vine. The central sacrament of the Christian church, holy communion, in which bread is eaten and wine is drunk[6], is a regular proclamation of our fundamental spiritual need and how it can be satisfied. More striking offers and claims from

Jesus are contained in the other metaphors—illumination for our path in a dark world; guidance, leadership and protection from the Good Shepherd[7], and the guarantee of fulfilled life here and after death. Finally, there is the most comprehensive statement of them all: that Jesus claims to be 'the way, the truth and the life'.

At this point we may well ask: if we are to take these claims seriously, how can we form a relationship with someone who lived in Palestine nearly 2,000 years ago, so far removed from us in both time and space? We find that question addressed in the Gospel of John. Before Jesus' death he promised that someone he called 'another Counsellor' would be with his followers to convince them of the reality of his presence and the truth of his teaching— God the Holy Spirit[8]. Christians have found it helpful to think of God as a Trinity: God the Father who is outside the world he created, God the Son who came and lived in the world as a human being, limited in time and space; and God the Holy Spirit who is not limited in this way, and who is God active and working in the world. It is the Holy Spirit who helps us[9] in our struggle to get to know God.

The two books
In this getting to know God, we have two main sources of information—the created universe on the one hand and the person of Jesus on the other. Those involved in the sixteenth-century reformation in the Western church and with the early days of the scientific revolution were well acquainted with these two sources. One of the most influential thinkers of those times was the philosopher Francis Bacon who, towards the end of his life became Lord Chancellor of England. 'Let no man think or maintain', he wrote, 'that a man can search too far or be too well studied in the book of God's word or in the book of God's works[10]'; a quotation reproduced by Charles Darwin on the flyleaf of *The Origin of Species*. In describing these two books he encapsulated the thinking that motivated many of the early scientists who were committed to their Christian faith as well as to their science; the idea he presented continues to be fundamental today.

From the book of nature (God's works) we learn of God's greatness, grandeur and consistency; from the person of Jesus presented in the Bible (God's word) we learn of his grace, love and purposes for human beings. Put these two views together and we begin, however dimly, to grasp the divine perspective. The God of our universe (and for all we know of other universes too) with its billions of galaxies, each with billions of stars in their different stages of evolution, the God of the living world with all its intimacy, variety and beauty, this same God is the one who has revealed himself through Jesus, the human being who (using another metaphor or model) is described as God's Son[11].

But now the question very naturally arises: what is the evidence for the picture we have presented? Is it all a pious invention? Are we not creating a God in our own image by extrapolation from our experience mixed with wishful thinking? What makes us sure of the objective existence of the spiritual dimension and of our perception of it?

Evidence for the spiritual dimension

There are three main lines of evidence: first, the historical record of the life, death and resurrection of Jesus; secondly, the universal and historical awareness of a spiritual dimension; thirdly, individual personal experience. I shall briefly look at these in turn.

Nearly all the historical evidence we have is contained in the documents of the New Testament. These have been carefully studied by historians, archaeologists and experts in linguistics and are generally believed to be genuine[12]. The various accounts of the life, death and resurrection of Jesus reinforce each other in the main, but differ in points of detail in ways which are often typical of eyewitness accounts.

Historical evidence on its own, however, can never be completely convincing. The records of the past are inevitably written with some particular perspective in mind. So far as we know, Jesus himself left no written record; the records we have were written by his disciples and followers quite deliberately from the standpoint of faith. Material was carefully selected and presented with the testimony of faith in mind[13].

Clearly, the disciples were convinced. Those converted to the Christian faith within weeks of the resurrection were convinced. Many of them, and many thousands since, have been sufficiently convinced to suffer and die for their faith. We may well ask the question, 'Why should we be convinced?'

Take, for instance, the central point: the resurrection of Jesus from death after he had been crucified (Fig. 10.1). The main objection to its truth arises from the feeling that an event so contrary to normal experience as a dead body coming alive again in resurrection requires far more than historical evidence for it to be accepted as fact[14]. People who have died just do not walk out of their tombs and then show themselves alive in different places. However strong the

FIG. 10.1 **The empty tomb.**

141

historical evidence may be (and many who have looked at it consider it to be very strong[15]), it cannot be strong enough to compensate for the completely unusual nature of the events.

Were it just a matter of academic debate, we might be happy to remain sceptical. But if Jesus really is God appearing as a human being[16], if he is God breaking into human history, if he is the way we get to know the greatest conceivable being, we look at the historical events in a different light and ask a different kind of question. We stop asking, 'How can I accept such unusual events as fact?' and

---

Jesus in the spiritual dimension

Let us go back to the two-dimensional world of Flatland and the attempt of the creature from Spaceland to convey the existence of the third dimension to the Flatland inhabitants (Fig. 10.2). The Spaceland creature not only demonstrated that it could see inside the Flatland houses and the Flatland beings themselves and describe in detail what was going on, but could also appear at will, albeit in a two-dimensional section, in any part of Flatland, and disappear at will.

Jesus after his resurrection also appeared and disappeared at will[17], demonstrating that he was no longer subject to the same limitations of space as he had been before.

The resurrection of Jesus and his post-resurrection appearances support his message, namely that there is a spiritual dimension of fundamental importance which can be discovered through him as 'the way, and the truth and the life'[18].

FIG. 10.2 A sphere from Spaceland over Flatland.

ask instead: 'Supposing they are fact, do they make sense in my experience of life?' In fact, we use the inductive method, first described in Chapter 1.

I shall return to the general question of miracles in Chapter 14. Here I wish to emphasize the particular point that, if Jesus is to convey the reality of eternal or spiritual life, if he is to demonstrate that evil and even death—the ultimate tragedy—cannot stop God's love for us[19], then his resurrection from death is the key to his whole message. There is a consistency between events in the life of Jesus (in particular the resurrection) and his teaching and declaration that he is the way to God.

The second line of enquiry comes through examination of the universal and historical human experience of the spiritual dimension. There is general evidence that most human beings, from whatever part of the world and from the earliest times, have exhibited a fundamental belief in a divine being or beings, and in some sort of spiritual world. More particularly so far as the claims of Christianity are concerned, there is the witness of millions of Christians over the years, whose lives have been transformed through contact with God and who claim the reality of a continued, living relationship with him through Jesus. Truth does not necessarily reside in the beliefs of large numbers or even a majority of people. But the experience of so many, especially the evidence of changed lives, may not be lightly dismissed.

A strong, historical case and the witness of millions of Christians cannot, however, convince me unless I have confirmation in my personal experience of the reality of a relationship with God. What sort of evidence must I look for?

A few, like the apostle Paul[20], experience it as a blinding light, illuminating in a moment the whole detailed landscape of faith. For most of us, however, the road to belief is a much longer one. As with most human relationships, it is not so much love at first sight, but a growing awareness of the reality of God.

It has certainly been that way with me. Brought up in a Christian home, I learned early in life the basic tenets of the Christian faith. The faith did not become my own until I realized that I could also meet the Jesus I read about in the pages of the Gospels through prayer and through the lives and conversations of others in the Christian community. Subsequently I have experienced a growing awareness and conviction of the reality of the spiritual dimension and of its relevance to all areas of life, including for instance my relationships and my professional scientific work.

The central features of the Christian religion, the death of Jesus on a cross—a criminal's death—and his resurrection to a life which cannot end, are events of particular relevance to me. Both mysterious and powerful, they provide the means whereby failure and sin can be forgiven and overcome.

As I have come to realize God's love not only for humanity in general but for me in particular, it has filled me with feelings of gratitude and worship. Like a jigsaw puzzle, seemingly unconnected pieces of life, thought and experience have begun to fit together. One jigsaw piece on its own cannot necessarily be understood as part of the picture on the front of the box; as a number of pieces have interlocked and a picture has begun to emerge, my conviction of the reality of the Christian message has become inescapable.

My argument is, therefore, that there is a coherence between the historical evidence, the experience of the church over the centuries and my own personal experience.

Given a position of faith, is the historical base of any importance? Some consider it of little relevance; faith, it is argued, can get along without its historical roots. For most Christians, however, myself included, the historical base is fundamental. Without it the whole structure falls to the ground. As Paul wrote, very early in the church's history: 'If Christ has not been raised, our preaching is useless and so is your faith.'[21] The historical base and the experience of faith go along together; neither is sustainable without the other.

Some may, however, without calling personal experience into question, still stumble over the central feature of Christianity. How, they ask, can anyone—even Jesus—be both God and human? Can science throw any light on this paradox?

Footnotes

1   For an exposition of this and other metaphors in the Gospel of John, see William Temple, *Readings in St John's Gospel*, Macmillan, 1961.

2   Psalm 33:6.

3   John 14:9.

4   John 8:56–59.

5   Matthew 4:4.

6   Luke 22:14–20, 1 Corinthians 11:23–29.

7   Jesus' Jewish listeners would have understood Jesus' claim to be the Good Shepherd as referring back to Ezekiel Chapter 34. In the light of Ezekiel 34:15, it amounts to a claim to be God.

8   John 14:16ff and 16:7–8.

9   The Greek word *paraklete*, often translated Counsellor, is also translated as Advocate or Strengthener. William Barclay, in his two-volume commentary on the Gospel of John (St Andrew Press, 1975), suggests that it could be translated 'Helper'.

10   F. Bacon, *The Advancement of Learning*, 1605, quoted by A.R. Peacocke, *Creation and the World of Science*, OUP, 1979, p3, who also expounds more of the historical background. Further details can also be found in C.A. Russell, *Cross-currents*, IVP, 1985.

11   Matthew 3:17; 4:3; John 1:49; 3:16; Hebrews 1:2.

12   See, for instance, P. Barnett, *Is the New Testament History?*, Hodder and Stoughton, 1986, and C. Blomberg, *The historical reliability of the Gospels*, IVP, 1987.

13   John 20:30–31.

14   For an evaluation of the importance of the resurrection, see G.E. Ladd, *I Believe in the Resurrection of Jesus*, Hodder and Stoughton, 1975.

15   See for instance Frank Morrison, *Who Moved the Stone?*, Faber and Faber/STL Books or Michael Green, *The Day Death Died*, IVP, 1982.f

16   1 Timothy 3:16.

17   Luke 24; John 20—21.

18   John 14:6

19   Matthew 9:6; John 3:16; 1 Corinthians 15:53–57; 2 Timothy 1:10; Hebrews 2:14.

20   Acts 9.

21   1 Corinthians 15:14

11 Waves, Particles and Incarnation

Two seemingly incompatible conceptions can each represent an aspect of the truth... they may serve in turn to represent the facts without ever entering into direct conflict.

L. V. DE BROGLIE

The nature of light

Three hundred years ago, the great scientist Isaac Newton thought a good deal about the nature of light. He carried out experiments, reflecting light from mirrors and refracting light through prisms, and came to the conclusion that all that he knew about light could be explained on the hypothesis that it consisted of a stream of particles.

About the same time, a Dutch scientist, Christiaan Huyghens, also pursued some elegant optical experiments and postulated that light consisted of waves. However, so strong was Newton's reputation that the scientific world took little notice of Huyghens' ideas.

A century later, Thomas Young reported the results of ingenious experiments demonstrating interference between two sources of light shining through a pair of slits. These strongly supported a wave theory of light. Even so, it was well into the nineteenth century before the wave theory was generally accepted, confirmation finally coming from the work of Clerk Maxwell, who elucidated the nature of the waves theoretically, showing that they were oscillations of coupled electric and magnetic fields.

So Newton was shown to have got it wrong and the wave theory reigned supreme—until the turn of the last century,

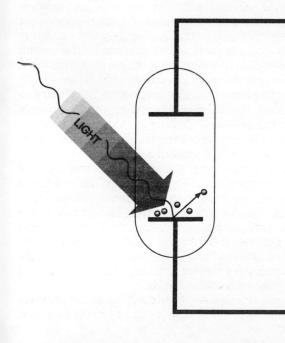

FIG. 11.1 Patterns known as Newton's rings produced by the interference between two beams of light. Such patterns demonstrate the wave nature of light—in the light areas, the two waves together make a bigger wave, while in the dark areas the two waves cancel each other out.

FIG. 11.2 The photoelectric effect. Light falling on a suitable surface causes electrons to be emitted which allow an electric current to pass through a circuit containing the photocell. This effect is a demonstration of the particle nature of light.

147

when various new observations of the photoelectric effect and of the nature of black-body radiation were made which did not fit into the wave picture at all, but suggested again that light consisted of particles.

The quantum theory of light, which postulates that light consists of streams of very small particles or 'quanta', was put forward by Max Planck in 1900 to explain these new facts, so beginning a remarkable revolution which completely transformed nineteenth-century physics.

But the question whether light was to be described as waves or as particles persisted. Some properties—diffraction and interference, for instance—were phenomena which could be associated only with waves (Fig. 11.1). On the other hand, the way in which light interacts with atomic systems, the photoelectric effect (Fig. 11.2) and the existence of discrete spectral lines could be described only in terms of particles. Different circumstances therefore required different and seemingly contradictory descriptions.

As the quantum theory developed, to some extent mathematics came to the rescue. Equations could be written down describing wave 'packets'—groups of waves localized in space as if they were particles. Then came Schrödinger's equation describing the wave nature of the behaviour of matter, and finally the equation formulated by Paul Dirac (see box in Chapter 4), which fitted together electromagnetic radiation and quantum mechanics in an extremely elegant way.

Dirac stuck firmly to his mathematical description, carefully avoiding the introduction of any pictorial model or mental picture of the phenomena described by his mathematical symbols; mental pictures, he explained, cannot be formed without introducing irrelevancies.

However, despite their limitations, mental pictures or physical models form an essential part of our scientific understanding. Although the duality inherent in the nature of light is accepted, and although we have a good idea under what circumstances the wave or the particle model can sensibly be applied, at the level of the model description, the paradox presented by the two contradictory models remains.

The person of Jesus

The dual description which is required of the nature of light can be employed as a parable of the paradox surrounding the person of Jesus. In the early centuries of the Christian era, a debate centred around theological schools in the two cities of Alexandria and Antioch, regarding how Jesus could be both God and a human being.

☐ The theologians at Alexandria emphasized particularly that Jesus was God. After all, they argued, his life clearly bore that out: his miracles, the authority with which he spoke. And did he not claim to be God, and was he not put to death on a charge of blasphemy?[1] How he could be truly human as well was their problem. The theologian Athanasius, for instance, argued that what Jesus knew as God, he pretended not to know in so far as he was human—an unsatisfactory solution.

☐ At Antioch, on the other hand, they emphasized particularly that Jesus was human. He became tired and hungry; he wept over the death of his friend Lazarus[2]. And how could he help us or represent us if he were not genuinely human? How could he be God as well? So at Antioch, they spoke of 'two natures'—God and human—in a kind of intimate cooperation.

So the debate went on between them. In the year 451 at the Council of Chalcedon, the original version of the Nicene Creed was reaffirmed in order to try to express a view of the incarnation which is true to the biblical picture of Jesus and to Christian experience. It reads:

We believe ... in one Lord Jesus Christ, the Son of God, begotten from the Father, only-begotten, that is, from the substance of the Father, God from God, light from light, true God from true God, begotten not made, of one substance with the Father, through whom all things came into being, things in heaven and things on Earth, who because of us and because of our salvation came down and became incarnate, becoming man ...'[3]

149

We can imagine the length of the committee meetings that produced that statement! But the debate did not stop at Chalcedon; it is, in fact, still going on.

Science and theology are full of paradoxical descriptions; in both, the language of description has many limitations, and reality can never be reduced to one particular model. It is perhaps not surprising that we have difficulty in trying to find adequate language to describe the behaviour of the elementary particles which make up an atom or an atomic nucleus. We should be even less surprised if we find difficulty in our attempts to describe the nature of the Deity. There are bound to be seeming contradictions and conflicts in the language we are forced to employ—but that does not imply the unreality of the underlying concepts. Truth and paradox can coexist,[4] as we will also find in the next chapter when I consider the vexed subject of petitionary prayer.

Footnotes

1 Mark 14:64.

2 John 11:35.

3 Quoted in J.N.D. Kelly, *Early Christian Creeds*, Longmans, 1960, pp 215–16.

4 A useful essay on the problems of language is by D.M. MacKay, 'What makes a contradiction?' in *The open mind and other essays*, IVP, 1988, pp 38–44.

PART 5
God in Action

C ontinuing the argument by induction, if we are in relationship with a God who is personal and has actually become one of us in order to form this relationship, what significance does this have for our lives? I will consider two areas where God and ordinary life come into close contact: what happens when we pray (Chapter 12), and the question of miracles (Chapter 13).

12 What Happens When We Pray?

More things are wrought by prayer than this world dreams of.
ALFRED LORD TENNYSON

In earlier chapters I considered God's activity in the world. An important way in which we relate to God and thus connect with that activity is through prayer. The practice of prayer as presented in the Bible and as experienced by Christians through the centuries presupposes a belief that God knows about, cares about and can take action regarding the matters being prayed about. In this chapter I consider how that connection is made both from our side and from God's side.

From our side, data comes from personal experience. I therefore begin by considering evidence both from the Bible and from modern times concerning the experience of people who pray. But trying to make sense of God's action in response to our prayer is more difficult. Can the analogy I have already used of God in the spiritual dimension be of help? How does the 'faith story' of the events in question relate to the 'scientific story' of those events? What problems does the use of this model raise? And can prayer be scientifically tested, or is a different kind of relationship involved?

Paul's injunction to pray without ceasing[1] highlights the importance of prayer in the life of the Christian. It points to two sorts of prayer, which I will call formal and informal prayer. Formal prayer consists of the set pieces and formulations of the kind used in church services and also in our regular private devotions. Informal prayers are those prayers, often short ones, often expressed silently, which we send up to God from anywhere at any time. They are the Christian's reactions to the variety of events that continually confront us. They may express thanks or adoration for something particularly good or beautiful; they may be requesting forgiveness for some failure or shortcoming. More often, however, they are 'asking' prayers pointing up a particular problem or a particular need of our own or of someone else. In any case, these informal prayers represent a continual attitude of mind. They are very much the way in which our relationship with God, as children dependent on a heavenly Father, is expressed and worked out in our day-to-day lives.

Praying for rain

What happens when we make these requests in prayer? Do we believe God listens to us? Do we believe God can do anything about our requests? Our attitude to prayer is bound to be influenced by what we believe about the way God acts in the world, which in turn is influenced by our scientific view. If we are Christian believers, the way we pray also affects the way we live. In addressing, therefore, the subject of petitionary or 'asking' prayer, we are addressing a matter of rather basic practical importance.

I should explain first that I do not consider myself an expert on prayer. I am not a particularly pious person by nature and the discipline of prayer does not come easily to me. I sometimes envy those to whom prayer seems natural, who without apparent difficulty spend an early morning hour each day in prayer. However, I am a practical person, and I want here to address real issues, not just theoretical ones, so I want to address squarely this question of what happens when we pray.

Those who are not believers see prayer, particularly prayers that ask for something, as wishful thinking. Although prayers are not always answered in the way requested, the believer will insist that they have been answered; 'No' or 'Not yet' can be valid answers so far as a Christian is concerned. No wonder, to the sceptic, praying appears to be something of a con! Because of this problem, some believers do not feel comfortable with 'asking' prayers; they feel that prayer should be confined to praise, worship, adoration, repentance and the process of aligning ourselves with the will of God. But is that an adequate view?

Because I am a meteorologist, I am often asked what I think about praying about the weather—for instance, praying for rain. If I believe that forecasts of tomorrow's weather are possible because it is dependent on processes in the atmosphere which can be described scientifically, how can I also believe that prayer can have anything to do with it? My answer is that I believe that it is entirely appropriate to pray about the weather, as it is about anything else that is of concern to us. But I also, as a scientist, believe that the movements of the atmosphere follow scientific laws. In Chapter 4 I spoke of two stories, the 'scientific story' (the one that is appropriate to weather forecasting) and the 'faith story' (the one that relates to my prayers). I explained that these two stories are complementary; the existence of the 'scientific story' in no way invalidates the 'faith story'. I suggested that our view of God should be big enough for us to believe that he can provide for consistency and reliability in both stories at the same time. I want to try and work out these ideas in more detail as they apply to our prayers.

Examples of prayer in the Bible

So that we have some data to consider, let us look at some particular examples of prayer. As we might expect, the Bible provides us with a good start. The great spiritual leaders of the Old Testament were all people of prayer (see box). Prayer was also a dominant theme in the life and teaching of Jesus, as described in the Gospels in the New Testament.

The early morning often found Jesus praying[2]. Two particular prayers of Jesus are recorded in detail: that in the garden of Gethsemane immediately before his death, when he requested, 'if it be possible', not to have to bear all the pain and suffering of the cross[3], and a prayer for his disciples[4]. Other shorter prayers are also recorded, one just before the raising of Lazarus from the dead[5].

Then there is the prayer which Jesus taught his disciples to pray, which we know as the Lord's Prayer[6]. Extremely

Some prayers of the Old Testament

Abraham was someone who lived so close to God that we find him not just pleading but arguing with God over the destruction of the cities of Sodom and Gomorrah[7]. His nephew Lot was in Sodom and Abraham wanted to save him. Even if there were only ten righteous people in Sodom, could God not spare the city, he argued? That particular prayer was not answered as Abraham wanted. Lot was saved but the cities were not spared.

There is also the lovely story of Abraham's servant being sent to look for a wife for Abraham's son Isaac[8]. As the servant and his camels were by the well at the town of Nahor in the region from where Abraham came, he asked God to give him a sign: that the girl whom he asked for a drink who would also water the camels would be the one he was looking for. And so it happened; Rachel was chosen to be Isaac's wife.

Many of David's prayers are preserved for us in the book of Psalms. All aspects of his life are included as he expresses to God his thoughts and feelings—even his deep remorse at having committed adultery with Bathsheba and having had her husband put to death[9]. His life was one of continual awareness of the presence of God, of God's provision for him and of his thorough dependence on God for help and for strength.

The prophet Elijah, too, was a giant in prayer. James, in his New Testament letter, describes him as someone like us![10] In order to provide a spiritual message to the people of Israel and their wicked king Ahab, he prayed for a period of drought. After three and a half years of drought, he prayed for rain, which came immediately after the dramatic contest between God and the pagan god Baal on Mount Carmel[11].

succinct in form, it covers the basic aspects of our relationship with God and with other people. Included within it is a request for the provision of our material needs: 'Give us today our daily bread.'

Jesus constantly emphasized that God provides for us in response to our asking. His statement: 'Ask and it will be given you[12],' was strengthened by an assurance that God cares and is willing to give. 'If you ... know how to give good gifts to your children,' Jesus said, 'how much more will your Father in heaven give good gifts to those who ask him[13]?' But we are to be persistent in prayer[14] just like children asking for something from their parents. God as our Father with us as his children is a model which Jesus continually offered as a pattern to govern our attitude in prayer. Trust in God's goodness and in his capacity to provide is a prerequisite for prayer to be answered. If they had faith enough, they could move mountains[15], Jesus told his disciples. And behind all his teaching on prayer Jesus reminded them of the extent and the detail of God's knowledge. 'Even the very hairs of your head are all numbered,'[16] he said!

Jesus also emphasized to his disciples the special value of corporate prayer. 'If two or three of you on Earth agree about anything you ask for,' he said[17], 'it will be done for you by my Father in heaven. For where two or three come together in my name, there I am with them.'

Prayer in the early church

Jesus' teaching on prayer has been reflected in the practice and experience of the church from early times until the present day. The early Christians felt that their work in the world was in partnership with God[18] and that they were utterly dependent on God for the means to carry it out[19]. Prayer was an essential weapon in the spiritual battle[20], and continual communication with God through prayer was a central link in the partnership. Praying together was particularly important to the early Christians[21]; they felt a strong connection between their corporate prayer, the presence of the Holy Spirit and their ability to speak out boldly as Christians [22].

Two modern examples: A) Financial provision

The history of the church abounds in accounts of those who have learnt completely to depend on and to trust in God, and who have found God supplying their needs and answering their requests in remarkable ways. For my first example, I have chosen the experience of George Müller[23] who was born in Prussia in 1805 and came to live in England in 1830. Here he settled as the minister of a church in Bristol, from where he carried on a variety of Christian enterprises which had influence worldwide. His most well-known work was on behalf of the orphans in and around Bristol, for whom, beginning in 1834, he set up a number of what became known after his death in 1898 as Müller's orphanages.

In setting up the orphan homes in 1834, Müller records that his reasons for so doing were not just to provide for the material and spiritual wellbeing of the orphans but also 'that God may be glorified in so furnishing means as to show that it is not a vain thing to trust in Him[24]'. He determined right from the start of the enterprise that he would not appeal directly or indirectly for funds or for other help but would rely solely on asking God. At no stage did he or others make known, outside a small trusted circle of coworkers, the state of the finances or the detailed needs of the orphanages. A summary annual report was all that the donors or the public were allowed to see. During the first sixty-four years of the orphan homes until Müller's death in 1898, over 10,000 orphans had been cared for and very close to £1 million (about £100 million in today's money) had been sent for their support[25]—all in answer to prayer.

A.T. Pierson's biography mentions a number of features that characterize Müller's record of these years in his journal.

☐ Firstly, there were experiences of frequent and prolonged financial straits. Often they were reduced to a single pound, a penny or nothing. Faith was kept in lively exercise, but was always rewarded, very often at the last minute. 'Not once or five times or five hundred times but thousands of times in these sixty years,' writes Müller, 'have we had in hand not enough for one more meal either in food or in funds, but not once has God failed us, not once have we or the orphans gone hungry or lacked any good thing[26].'

☐ Secondly, there is constant emphasis on 'reliance on the unseen God and nothing else'. Müller regularly exercised extreme caution lest there should be any careless betrayal of pressing need to the outside public. Several examples illustrate this well. In 1847 at a time of great need, the regular annual statement was withheld in case it could be construed as an appeal for aid[27]. In reply to a supporter who urged Müller to send him details of what was needed for work, again at a time of great need,

Müller replied he could not tell him, 'as the primary object of the work in my hands is to lead those who are weak in faith to see that there is reality in dealing with God alone[28]'. Further, we are told that friends who asked for information about whether their gifts had come at a particularly opportune time were not given the information but merely referred to the statements contained in the next annual report[29].

☐ Thirdly, there is the constant experience of the working of God upon the minds, hearts and consciences of contributors to the work so that needed funds were forthcoming[30]. Referring to Müller's journal, Pierson writes:

It will amply repay one to ... trace the hand of God touching the springs of human action all over the world in ways of His own, and at times of great need, and adjusting the amount and the exact day and hour of supply, to the existing want. Literally from the Earth's ends, men, women and children who have never seen Mr Müller and could have known nothing of the pressure of the time, have been led at the exact crisis of affairs to send aid in the very sum or form most needful. In countless cases, while he was on his knees asking, the answer has come in such close correspondence with the request as to shut out chance as an explanation, and compel belief in a prayer-hearing God.

Not surprisingly Pierson also comments on Müller's growing boldness of faith in asking and trusting for great things.

I have chosen to describe the experience of George Müller because of the scale of his enterprise and also because of the careful records which he kept of his experiences of God's answers to prayer. I do not doubt the accuracy of his accounts; he was clearly meticulous in the way he kept his records.

Many Christian believers and Christian workers over the centuries have similar stories to tell, although perhaps not involving work on such a scale or being so carefully recorded. On a very much smaller scale of faith—although, I believe, of a similar kind—I can recall several occasions when some of us involved in setting up a Christian enterprise in Oxford, the North Oxford Overseas Centre, in the 1960s and 1970s, had similar experiences. Necessary resources were provided through what seemed to us remarkable answers to prayer.

B) Physical disability

A large number of asking prayers are concerned with physical or mental sickness or disability. Many examples exist of those who have been able to overcome and rise above their sickness and disabilities. For my second modern example of prayer, I have chosen Joni Eareckson Tada.

In 1967, when she was seventeen, she dived by mistake into shallow water in Chesapeake Bay and broke her neck. Since then she has been a quadriplegic, paralyzed in her arms and legs, and has undergone periods of long and painful treatment. Joni is a particularly shining example of someone who through prayer has been able not only to come to terms with her condition but also to see its effect in transforming her life [31].

After an initial period of learning to cope with her paralysis, Joni, encouraged by some of her Christian friends, found it hard to believe that it was God's will for her to continue in a paralyzed state and began to look for 'miraculous' healing. After all, was not a significant part of the ministry of Jesus concerned with healing people, especially paralyzed people? She and many of her friends prayed for her healing; a specific occasion of 'laying on of hands' and anointing with oil [32] was arranged. She firmly believed that she had faith in God and expected to be healed. But there was no change in her condition and those prayers were not answered in that way.

However, although still suffering from her disability she would now say unequivocally that her prayers and those of her friends have been answered. So much so that she writes:

Today as I look back, I am convinced that the whole ordeal of my paralysis was inspired by God's love. I wasn't a rat in a maze. I wasn't the brunt of some cruel divine joke. God had reasons behind my suffering, and learning some of them has made all the difference in the world.

Joni outlines some of the reasons. One is clearly the way in which she sees her ministry to thousands of others, especially those suffering from acute disabilities. She explains [33] that one of God's purposes has been to sensitize her to people she would never have been able to relate to otherwise.

A second reason is the way in which it brings glory to God and the evidence it provides of what God's grace and power can do in a life. 'When a Christian shows faith and love for his Maker,' she writes [34], 'in spite of the fact that, on the surface, it looks as if he's been forgotten, it does say something impressive. It shows the scoffers that our God is worth serving even when the going gets tough. It lets a sceptical world know that what the Christian has is real.' She is a remarkable demonstration of how 'God's power is made perfect in weakness.' [35]

But Joni goes on to describe a third and perhaps even more powerful reason which is about what her suffering has done for her, her understanding of God and the deepening of her relationship with him. She writes, 'My paralysis has drawn me close to God and given a spiritual healing which I wouldn't trade for a hundred active years on my feet.' [36]

Healing: medical and spiritual

In the context of Joni's story, it is appropriate to consider further the question of prayers for healing. To write about spiritual healing as Joni does seems to many to miss the point. Is not healing concerned with physical recovery? When we pray for healing, is it not physical healing that we generally mean? And where does the practice of medicine come in?

Healing featured strongly in the ministry of Jesus and has always been a concern of the Christian church. Christian missionaries have been pioneers in bringing medical aid and healing to all parts of the world. Many of our prayers today for ourselves or for others are also concerned with health and healing. How can we expect God to act in response to such prayers?

The first point to make here is that much healing today occurs through medicine. I remember a colleague of mine telling me that his son had just been ill from pneumonia. 'Years ago,' he said, 'we would have been praying over the boy for weeks; now, thanks to antibiotics he is completely better after two or three days. Penicillin,' he commented, 'is worth an awful lot of prayer!'

A remark like that expresses a completely false dichotomy. It suggests that prayer and medicine have nothing to do with each other. The same dichotomy is sometimes presented by those within the church (where in recent years there has been a renewed interest in 'miraculous' healing as part of the church's proper activity) who contrast 'miraculous' or 'faith' healing, seen as the work of God, with the application of medicine, seen as a purely human activity. Such a view is not only misleading; it is at variance with a belief in God as creator and sustainer of the natural order.

Medical means, being derived from God's creation, are very much the works of God. Doctors often see their role as one of co-operation with God, especially as they increasingly realize the importance of treating the whole person. They cannot be concerned only with the body and its biochemistry; complete healing involves the whole person: body, mind and relationships with others, including, I would argue, with God.

Such complete healing was often evident in the healing ministry of Jesus[37]. The Christian community should therefore be working together with doctors to provide a more complete healing ministry; our prayers for healing should address the whole person and all the resources God has provided for the purposes of healing. Some of the most striking modern 'miracles' are those in which both bodily and spiritual healing have occurred together, and I will return to the question of 'miraculous' healing in the next chapter.

Analyzing the data

What does all this data on prayer add up to, particularly in the context of our considerations here: an inductive argument in the search for God?

Prayer is, of course, such a personal and complex experience that it is bound to be difficult, if not impossible, to delineate its boundaries. Let me, however, make some summarizing points.

☐ Firstly, for Christians, prayer is an expression of their relationship with God. It is the means whereby they, as God's children, communicate with God as their Father; how he speaks to them and they to him. Because of this close relationship prayer is never far away. It is an attitude of mind through which they continually attempt to discover the will of God and to act upon it.

☐ Secondly, prayer involves a lot of asking—asking for things personal to each individual, for 'daily bread', for forgiveness, for healing in all senses of that word, for strength to overcome temptation and to face problems. The asking will also involve things concerned with God's work in the world, for his kingdom to come and his will to be done—for instance, for other people and their needs and relationships, for national and world problems.

☐ Thirdly, prayer must not be confused with magic. It is not 'rubbing the magic lamp' and making wishes. The answers to our requests may not be what we expect or would like, and God answers similar prayers by different people in very different ways. The centre and purpose of prayer is to align our wills with God's will and to couple our efforts to serve God with his energy and strength.

☐ Fourthly, the exercise of trust is basic to the exercise of prayer. There is no point in praying if we do not believe (however shaky that belief may sometimes be) that God knows of, cares about and can take action relating to the subjects of our prayers.

162

☐ Fifthly, prayer involves other people. Corporate prayer in twos or threes or larger groups can be particularly valuable in enabling praying Christians to be effective partners with others in the pursuit of God's work in the world. And answers to prayer are most commonly mediated through the actions of other people.

☐ Finally, prayers for healing should address the healing of the whole person and all the resources available for healing, including medical resources.

How does God respond to prayer?

In Chapter 9, I introduced the analogy of the spiritual dimension outside the three dimensions of space and one dimension of time to help us to understand where God is in relation to his universe, and how God acts in the world. Let me first explain how I believe the analogy or model of the spiritual dimension can help us understand what happens when we pray. We shall then consider some of the many problems and questions which are inevitably raised by the idea and the practice of prayer.

Our prayers go to God in the spiritual dimension. He is able to take them and use them to influence events in our world at different points of space and time (Fig. 12.1). So far as we are concerned, these events constitute the 'faith story' associated with our prayers. In responding to our prayers, therefore, God is not constrained by space and time in the same way that we would be in responding to action by others. God has freedom to act at every time and place—in the past as well as in the present and in the future. 'Before they call I will answer,'[38] God says of his people.

Let me take an example from the story of George Müller. On 9 March 1842 the situation at the orphanage was completely desperate, resources being completely exhausted[39]. Prayers were made for provision. The morning post came with no relief. However, at the latest possible moment, a letter at first wrongly delivered arrived, with a gift for £10 from someone living in Dublin. The answer to those morning prayers began some days before

FIG. 12.1 **God is able to take our prayers outside the dimensions of our world and to use them to influence events in our world at different points of space and time.**

in Dublin; it involved the donor, the postal service and various modes of transport culminating in the arrival of the cheque at the crucial moment. Thousands of similar instances occur in Müller's story.

As a particular result of this view, consider a problem sometimes experienced by a person who wants to pray, say, at the end of the day, about an event which has occurred during that day. The outcome of that event, although unknown to the praying person, will already have been determined. Does prayer after the event make any sense?

Realizing that prayer is communication with God who is not constrained as we are by time, we can say that such prayer is entirely appropriate. In saying that, I need to add, of course, that were the outcome of the event already known to the praying person, it would be of no use to pray for a change to that outcome; prayer cannot alter events which in our time frame have already occurred.

I have been considering the 'faith story'. How about the 'scientific story'? We argued earlier that God is big enough and clever enough to maintain at the same time the consistency of both 'faith' and 'scientific' stories. But I am bound to ask the question: is there always this consistency, or is the natural order of things sometimes disturbed? In a particular case of an answer to prayer associated with significant events in the 'faith story', would a scientist with access to all the facts recognize anything unusual or inconsistent in the 'scientific story'? The person who prayed may describe the events as 'miraculous', but would 'miraculous' be a correct description of the 'scientific story'?

In practice, of course, we never know enough to rule out that possibility. But, in most cases, the significance in the 'faith story' arises from the actions or choices of particular people or from unusualness in the timing or in the sequences or juxtaposition of events, more than in the events themselves. Significance or unusualness in the 'faith story' does not necessarily imply unusualness in the 'scientific story'. I am not saying that miracles in the scientific sense cannot occur (those are the subject of the next chapter), but I am arguing that a description of events as unusual or 'miraculous' is normally to do with the structure of the 'faith story' rather than the 'scientific story'.

Very frequently the agents in the 'faith story' are people. Stories like those of George Müller are built around the cooperative actions of many people, influenced by God. Often these are people who themselves pray either alone or together (I have already explained the value of corporate prayer) and, to a greater or lesser degree, can be said to be in tune with God and his purposes. 'Faith stories' are built up through the thoughts and activities of many people cooperating with God in his work in the world.

In his choice of agents, however, it would seem that God is not limited to those who are consciously in tune with him. The provision of resources for the Müller orphanages, for instance, involved not just the donors but all those who took part in the transmission of the gifts.

Examples also abound in the Bible of God making use of those who are not conscious of a role as one of his agents. The prophet Isaiah sees Cyrus, king of Persia, as one chosen by God to bring to an end the exile of the Israelites in Babylon[40]. In the New Testament, Jesus described those responsible for his arrest and crucifixion as unwittingly carrying out God's purposes[41]; a theme taken up later by the leaders of the early church[42]. The crucifixion of Jesus is presented as the supreme example of God's ability to transform great evil and seeming tragedy into even greater good, and this continual process of transformation is central to much of God's plan for human beings.

This attempt to apply the analogy of the spiritual dimension to the practice of prayer raises a number of questions, which I now consider.

Does God know the future?

We have seen that in response to our particular requests in prayer God sets up chains of events which may begin years before the particular request is made. In illustrating this with the model of the spiritual dimension (in what some might feel a somewhat cavalier manner), we have assumed that, for God, all constraints of time have been removed and that past, present and future are all transparent to him and available for his action.

That implies that God can see the future as a whole, something which we should expect from One who is the creator of time as well as space, who is the basis of the creation's existence and whom we have described as the greatest conceivable being. But if God knows the future, is the future determined? If it is, what has happened to human free will—is that then an illusion?

Here we come up against our limited understanding of our own minds, and the extreme limitations we are bound to have as we attempt to describe God. We must tread cautiously and reverently, but as we saw in Chapter 9, that need not stop us trying to come up with descriptions and models that help. In that chapter I emphasized how God is both immanent and transcendent with respect to time and we drew a distinction between God-within-time and God-outside-time. For us, who experience the 'before' and 'after' which result from the flow of time, and also for God-within-time, the future cannot be completely determined; events are to come in the future which depend on free human decisions yet to be made[43]. The nature of the freedom which we as God's creatures have been given and the whole idea of God-within-time mean that God has limited himself[44] in order to allow us that freedom and in order to experience with us the pain, the suffering—and the pleasures—of our human existence.

Are there limitations to prayer?

If we believe God to be great and all-powerful we may feel that there should be no limitations on God's power to answer prayer. Can we ask for things clearly outside the normal scientific order? After all, Jesus talked of mountains being moved[45] and reminded his disciples that 'with God all things are possible'.[46] When it comes to asking, just as a child may ask a parent, the nature of prayer is such that there need be no limitations. But what about our expectations in reply to our requests? Our perspective here is determined by our knowledge of the life of Jesus and by our knowledge of the experience of others as well as of our own.

It is notable that Jesus, despite the latent power which was available to him, did not interfere capriciously with the natural order[47]. Apart from miracles of healing, miracles in the sense of events outside the normal scientific order are surprisingly rare in his life. The turning of water into wine[48] and the miraculous feeding of crowds on hillsides in Galilee[49] are the main examples. Although in these events Jesus was responding to a clear need, they also have something of a unique character about them; they were seen as signs[50] providing authentication of his person and his message. Well-attested records of such events are also rare in the history of the church through the centuries and in our experience today.

Although, therefore, as part of the dialogue we have with God in prayer we may ask for similar events today, we will not expect God to act in this way as a matter of routine. As we emphasized earlier, the Christian will be looking for evidence of God's activity in the normal circumstances of life, not so much in the 'scientific story' as in the 'faith story'—an emphasis expressed by the biblical writers in both Old and New Testaments who frequently describe God's provision for us through his normal activity[51].

In some events, seeing consistency in the 'faith story' as well as in the 'scientific story' will be relatively easy. This is not, however, always the case. The Christian believer is often faced with circumstances which seem difficult to understand. Sometimes, taken from almost any point of view, they appear wrong, and prayers do not always seem to be answered.

It is on these occasions that sceptical scientists, to whom this 'faith talk' appears in any case as wishful thinking, if not nonsense, are at their most critical. Belief in an overall consistent plan hardly seems supported by the facts.

A related question is why prayer does not seem to be more effective. The question may be put like this: 'I can see that God seems to answer specific individual prayers of particular people, but how about all the prayers for peace, for the cessation of violence and gross inhumanity, for the relief of famine or distress on a large scale. Why are not these prayers answered?'

Immediately the more general question is raised as to why God, if all-good and all-powerful, allows evil and suffering to continue largely unchecked—probably the most fundamental and difficult question faced by any religion. I cannot address the general question here (though I refer to it again in Chapter 13). What I can do is to refer to the words of the Lord's Prayer in which we are encouraged to pray for God's kingdom to come and for God's will to be done[52]. In the exercise of prayer we are cooperating with God—and God invites us to so cooperate—in his work of overcoming evil in all its forms. John Polkinghorne[53] employs the example of resonance (oscillations in synchronization with each other) to illustrate prayer, which is at its most powerful when God's will and our will are tuned together in mutual resonance.

Several further points can be made.

☐ First, it is important to remember that, while in the scientific description we are dealing with impersonal matters, in the 'faith' description we are confronted by a personal God and concerned with a relationship in which trust is a vital element, just as children will trust their parents even when they do not understand a situation.

☐ Secondly, we are bound to realize that our knowledge of God's overall plan is inevitably extremely limited. A junior infantry officer engaged in a battle may be puzzled by his particular instructions; he will possess very limited knowledge as to where his part of the action fits into the overall strategy of the battle.

In a similar way, if I am a participant in God's plan, there cannot fail to be an element of mystery about where my small world and limited capability fit into it. God being so great, his plan will be grand and comprehensive far beyond the limits of my imagination.

☐ Thirdly, it does appear that the greater the trust and the deeper the commitment, the greater the degree of understanding which is given. The eighteenth-century poet, William Cowper, who was often given to deep depression, wrote a poem which begins:

God moves in a mysterious way
His wonders to perform.

He goes on to affirm:

Deep in unfathomable mines
Of never failing skill
He treasures up his bright designs
And works his sovereign will.

Blind unbelief is sure to err
And scan his works in vain.
God is his own interpreter
And he will make it plain.

Can prayer be tested?

An important question which a scientist, when confronted with prayer, will raise is whether answers to prayer can be tested. If so, can we thereby demonstrate the reality of God's work in the world? Can an experiment similar to an experiment in science be carried out to see if prayer works?

Sir Francis Galton, a scientist particularly interested in human intelligence, attempted such a test towards the end of last century, by looking at the mortality statistics for royal personages and clergy. Since, he considered, these were the people most prayed for, they might be expected to live longer than others. He found no statistical effect and concluded that prayer was an ineffective superstition.

There are two main problems with such testing of the efficacy of prayer.

☐ Firstly, it is not possible to set up simple tests of God's response to prayer requests. Answers to prayer do not come in the form of a simple mechanical-type response. As we have seen, they may not be what we either wanted or expected. If they were simple and automatic, we would be dealing not with prayer but with something more like magic—a power to exercise control over the course of nature. But prayer is not a mechanical device; it is the activity of a relationship.

We can compare the endeavour of 'testing' prayer with the problem of applying scientific tests to our normal human relationships. As C.S. Lewis points out[54], the response to requests in the context of our day-to-day dealings with each other is often also complex. Even if we get what we ask for, it is not necessarily easy to prove a causal connection between the asking and the getting. Relationships cannot be tested by asking questions which have simple yes/no answers.

☐ Secondly, the type of evidence which might be produced regarding answers to prayer is unlikely to be convincing to those who want to remain sceptical. If we look at the sort of examples of answers to prayer which I described earlier, which involved what appear to be remarkable coincidences in the way resources were provided for a

Christian enterprise, I would want to argue, for instance in the case of Müller, that the sheer weight of evidence over the years adds up to something substantial. However, although individual instances are striking and many put together add further strength to the case, the sceptic can always argue that coincidences and unusual healings occur when prayer is not involved.

The quality and veracity of the evidence can also be questioned; for instance, just how rigorous was Müller in practice in keeping financial information within the house? Unless sceptics are prepared to assess the whole consistency of the 'faith story' (which presupposes a relationship or a predisposition to a relationship with God) they may well not be convinced—just as the walker in Chapter 1 who found a tortoise would be unlikely to take it as evidence of a Designer of the universe without other experience of such a God.

The problem of proof is illustrated well by events in the life and ministry of Jesus, where we find two quite different types of situation. Some of Jesus' miracles are to be seen as signs[55] authenticating who he was. In other cases, especially in some of the healings, Jesus gave strict instructions that there should be no publicity[56]. When some of the leaders of the day asked him for a sign or a miracle, Jesus did not oblige[57]. He knew that they were not really serious and commented that if they failed to believe Moses and the prophets, they would not believe him even if confronted by someone risen from the dead[58]. In contrast, however, people in need who came believing he could help them found their need met[59].

Although, therefore, simple scientific tests are bound to be somewhat flawed from the start, prayer can be tested in the much more complex way that the partners in a relationship test the genuineness of that relationship. A particular prayer request may involve an individual Christian or the Christian community. The testing of the answer to that request will usually be of a nature that is personal to the individual or the community. Because making the prayer to start with presupposes some sort of relationship, the answer to it may be difficult to explain to others outside that relationship. It is, however, the positive results from such tests which enable the relationship to grow.

Drawing conclusions

Let me summarize some of the points I have made in applying the analogy of the spiritual dimension to the practice of prayer.

☐ I have stressed God's transcendence and immanence with respect to both space and time; he is both outside and within space and time. This means that in response to our prayers God acts without the constraints of space and time.

☐ God often works through people as his agents.

☐ God has limited himself in order to allow us freedom and to be involved with us in all parts of our lives, including our pain and suffering.

☐ We should look for significance and the possibility of the unusual and the miraculous in the 'faith story' rather than in the 'scientific story'.

☐ In prayer we are cooperating with God in his work in the world. The transformation into good of events and of human actions is a central component of this.

☐ The possibility of 'scientific' proof of the results of prayer is bound to be limited because prayer is a relationship; the tests we apply must be appropriate to a relationship.

Prayer is a tremendous privilege and an exciting challenge. I have no doubt at all that we completely underestimate its value and effect. Talking about prayer and trying to understand it, however, does not move us very far forward. What really matters is doing it.

Footnotes

1   1 Thessalonians 5:17.
2   Mark 1:35.
3   Mark 14:32–42.
4   John 17.
5   John 11:41–42.
6   Matthew 6:9–13.
7   Genesis 18:16–33.
8   Genesis 24.
9   Psalm 51.
10 James 5:17.
11 1 Kings 17, 18.
12 Matthew 7:7.
13 Matthew 7:11.
14 Luke 11:5–8.
15 Matthew 21:21.
16 Matthew 10:30.
17 Matthew 18:19–20.
18 Acts 2:42, 4:10, 6:8.
19 Acts 4:23–31, Philippians 4:13.
20 Ephesians 6:18.
21 Acts 3:42, 4:23ff, 12:12ff, 20:36, 21:5.
22 Acts 4:31.
23 For a biography see A.T. Pierson, *George Müller of Bristol*, Pickering and Inglis, 1972.
24 *loc. cit.*, p 121.
25 *loc. cit.*, p 298.
26 *loc. cit.*, p 79.
27 *loc. cit.*, p 80.
28 *loc. cit.*, p 164.
29 *loc. cit.*, p 338.
30 *loc. cit.*, p 79.
31 *J. Eareckson & S. Estes, A step further*, Pickering and Inglis, 1978.
32 As suggested by James 5:14.
33 *loc. cit.*, p 17.
34 *loc. cit.*, p 36.
35 2 Corinthians 12:9.
36 *loc. cit.*, p 158.
37 See, for instance, Mark 2:1–12; John 5:1–15; John 9.
38 Isaiah 65:24.
39 A.T. Pierson, *loc. cit.*, p 179.

40 Isaiah 45.

41 Luke 22:22; John 19:11.

42 Acts 2:23.

43 W.S. Anglin, *op. cit.*, pp 80–81, develops an argument using formal logic that God's foreknowledge does not imply that future events are determined.

44 See P. Fiddes, *op. cit.*

45 Matthew 17:20.

46 Mark 6:27.

47 Matthew 4:1–11.

48 John 2:1–11.

49 John 6:1–13.

50 For instance, the signs in John's Gospel.

51 Psalm 104; Matthew 6:11, 26, 30.

52 Matthew 6:10.

53 J. Polkinghorne, *Science and Providence, loc. cit.*, Chapter 6.

54 C.S. Lewis, 'The efficacy of prayer', in *Fern-seed and elephants*, Collins Fount Paperbacks, 1977.

55 For instance, the signs in John's Gospel.

56 Mark 5:43.

57 Matthew 16:3; Luke 23:8.

58 Luke 16:31.

59 Luke 4:38, 5:13, 7:1–6, 18:42.

13 Natural or Supernatural?

If they do not listen to Moses and the prophets, they will not be convinced even if someone rises from the dead.
JESUS IN LUKE 16:31

After quarks, believing in the virgin birth is a doddle.
CAPTION TO CARTOON IN *NEW SCIENTIST*

I have elaborated on the faith story and its relation to prayer; but prayer is a notoriously subjective experience. Does God intervene in the world in an objectively verifiable way?

Where can miracles fit in to the scheme of things I have presented? Does it make sense to talk of God intervening in particular events? I also want to return to the question I began to address in Chapter 7, of God's action in the world and to what extent we can discern the existence of God's plan.

In previous chapters I have continually emphasized that God is at work in the natural world, that it is God's moment-by-moment activity that is maintaining the universe in being. With this picture in view, does not the suggestion that God might 'intervene' in the natural world seem superfluous? He is already there all the time. The experience of scientists and the expectation of believers in God the Creator and Sustainer is that the natural world should demonstrate an extremely high degree of orderliness, consistency and stability. Where then is there room, if indeed there is, for miracles?

First, we need to ask just what we mean by a miracle. Clearly we mean an unusual or striking event, but not just that. Many unusual events may arouse our curiosity, we may remark, 'How odd!'—but we would not describe them as miraculous. In order to be classed as a miracle, an event must have significance apart from its being unusual. It must convey a message to the person or persons involved. The message may be to do with God's providence—a 'miraculous' escape or unusual provision of some kind—or it may be related to a particular physical or spiritual need, or to guidance regarding a future decision or action.

Two kinds of miracles

In considering the occurrence of miracles, it is convenient to divide miraculous events into two categories, dependent on how they might be viewed by a scientific observer.

☐ Firstly, there are those happenings which, because of their timing or unusual character, have a particular significance for an individual or for a group of people, but in which a scientist would not find anything ano-malous from the strictly scientific point of view, or anything outside conventional scientific experience. Events of this kind have already been considered in several of the previous chapters, where I have continu-ally emphasized the importance of the 'faith story' as well as the 'scientific story'. For the religious believer the presence of significance in the 'faith story' is a normal experience. The significance can be much enhanced if the happenings also appear unusual; in which case they may be referred to as miraculous; I refer to them as miracles of the first kind.

Some believers would also call them supernatural. However, to refer to them in this way is, I believe misleading. They are completely natural events. We have argued that God is at work all the time in all events; if our 'faith eyes' were more sensitive we might perceive more significance in all the normal happenings of life.

☐ Secondly, there are events which, again, have particular significance, but which it is likely that a scientific observer (if present with appropriate equipment) would have concluded were scientifically anomalous and not in agreement with known scientific law. I shall call them miracles of the second kind. It is these events of the second kind which I particularly address in this chapter.

Miracles in the life of Jesus

Many of the miracles in the life of Jesus as recorded in the gospels fit into this second category. Most of them were connected either with the person of Jesus (his virgin birth, his rising from death, his appearances after death and his return to God), with healing (including three instances of people being raised from the dead), or with the provision of need (for instance, the feeding of the five thousand or the turning of water into wine).

Scientists are bound to be sceptical about such events because they are anomalous and do not fit into the normal scientific pattern. From the strictly scientific point of view such events would be dismissed as most unlikely, if not impossible. But scientists are also bound to pay particular attention to seeming anomalies in case something of importance has been missed. Do they, for instance, have a wider significance?

Investigation of the unexplained is one of the major methods of scientific advance. Let me give two examples (see box): the unexpected fogging of photographic plates which led to Henri Becquerel's discovery of radioactivity, and the observations of perturbations in the orbits of the planets Uranus and Neptune which led to the discovery of

---

Investigating the unexplained: a major means of scientific discovery

In 1896 Henri Bequerel was working in Paris, investigating the properties of phosphorescent substances giving off X-rays. He placed them on photographic plates covered with black paper and exposed them to sunlight. He reported his results to the Academy of Sciences in Paris and demonstrated that shadows of coins could be formed on the plates. One week after his presentation to the Academy, he found that uranium salts continued to fog the plates even though they were no longer exposed to sunlight.

His further investigation of this observation led to the discovery of radioactivity.

Percival Lowell in 1915 carefully studied observations of small perturbations in the orbits of Uranus and Neptune, and predicted the existence of another planet beyond Neptune. It was not, however, until 1930 that telescope observations confirmed his predictions. The new planet was named Pluto—the first two letters of the new name being Lowell's initials.

---

the planet Pluto. In a similar way, with regard to the unusual events during the ministry of Jesus, it is necessary to ask whether they are conveying a particular message of which we need to take notice.

Let us look therefore at the particular significance of the miracles of Jesus. They were seen by the Gospel writers, especially by John, as signs[1], whose purpose was not only to meet a particular need but to authenticate the message Jesus came to bring. This message was that Jesus himself possessed a unique relationship to God (he is portrayed as both God and human) and that he came to demonstrate God's compassion, love and forgiveness towards all people, demonstrated by his miracles of healing and provision.

When I speak of the miracles as authentication of Jesus' message, I do not mean that they were meant as knock-down or 'laser' miracles (as Dr David Jenkins, the former Bishop of Durham has called them), calculated by their very nature to force people into belief. That was not the way Jesus taught and worked[2]. What I am arguing is that, when looked at in the context of his life and message, there is something fitting about these miraculous events. The events are interpreted by Jesus' message, which in turn is reinforced by the events. .

As we saw in Chapter 10 when considering Jesus' resurrection, we can readily argue that if Jesus really is God, we would expect unusual events to be associated with his coming. On the other hand, how about the stress I have placed, based on scientific experience and belief in an orderly creator, on the stability and orderliness of the natural world? If we accept New Testament miracles, is not our belief in the consistency of the universe destroyed? I do not think that it is.

Let us go back again to the Flatland illustration of Chapter 9. To the Flatlanders, the appearance of a sphere from Spaceland was unusual and inconsistent with Flatland science. But looked at from the further perspective of the third dimension, it was entirely consistent. Further, a demonstration of that kind was necessary if the Flatlanders were to have any inkling of the existence of the third dimension.

We can look at miraculous events in the life of Jesus in a similar way. From the strictly scientific point of view they are anomalous. However, in science the interesting anomaly can be an important lead in pointing to the way forward. Similarly, in our view of the events associated with the life of Jesus, it is necessary to balance their anomalous character and their apparent scientific inconsistency against the broader consistency which appears when we look from the perspective of the spiritual dimension.

Consider the problem Jesus faced in getting his message across. It would have been futile for him to claim to have a special relationship with the creator of the universe, to be divine himself, if he failed to demonstrate the claim through actions as well as words. Jesus made precisely this point when he claimed for himself God's prerogative to forgive, and demonstrated deity by healing a man with paralysis[3]. His actions were relevant to his message and appropriate to the expectations of the time in which he lived.

Standing back and looking at the teaching of Jesus about God's love, compassion and provision, we find a fitness in his actions, be they ordinary or miraculous, which gives credence to his teaching. We need such windows into the spiritual dimension if we are to take it seriously.

When this view is taken, it may seem surprising that the life of Jesus was not surrounded by many more miracles and unusual events. As we read the Gospel stories, there seems to be a measured restraint. Remember Jesus was fully human as well as fully divine (see Chapter 11). He accepted completely the limitations of a human existence and rejected out of hand temptations to throw those limitations overboard in order to serve himself[4]. Nowhere can this be seen more forcibly than when Jesus approached his death, realizing that there were means instantly available for him to avoid the shame, the pain and the cruelty of being crucified[5]. However, because of his determination to accomplish God's grand plan, he allowed himself to be cruelly put to death. As Sir Robert Boyd, one of the scientific pioneers in space research, has rather poignantly put it, 'God holds the iron rigid and the cross upright as we impale His Son.'[6]

Resurrection

Any Christian consideration of the subject of miracles is bound to focus on the events at the centre of the Christian message—the death and resurrection of Jesus. Based on the resurrection of Jesus, Christians believe and hope in the resurrection of the body after death. What do Christians mean by resurrection?

What they do not mean is just the continuation beyond death of some part of me that I call my soul or my spirit. Much more than that is implied.

An analogy I find helpful is based on the computer. Computer hardware consists of silicon chips, wires, disk and tape stores, keyboards and tape decks with which the input can be introduced, and screens and printers which display the output. The computer software consists of programs, which manipulate (and in sophisticated computers learn from) the input data and provide the means to organize the output and the contents of the data store. The software is of no use by itself; it needs hardware on which to act and through which to be expressed.

Computer hardware has a limited life; in time it wears out. Software is not so perishable—it can be transferred to new hardware, although it will still bear characteristics of the hardware for which it was originally written. New, more advanced hardware can provide more scope for the software, not only enabling larger calculations to be carried out more efficiently, but perhaps providing new capabilities.

Our bodies are like hardware, providing input devices (our senses) and output devices (our limbs, speech and so on), a processor and storage (our brains). Some software is built in from the start; it is genetically determined. Other software is continuously generated throughout our lives from interaction with our environment, with other people, from our thought processes and our choices and from interaction with the hardware.

Our bodies, in due course, like any other hardware, wear out. In resurrection, the Christian hope is for a new body which will have sufficient continuity with the old to take on board all the relevant parts of the old software and to give us new means of expression[7]. Because in the resurrection life we will be with God in a much closer way, the spiritual dimension will be especially important. Of particular relevance, therefore, will be the software developed over the course of our lives which relates to our experience of God.

All this may sound somewhat like a runaway dose of wishful thinking—'pie in the sky when we die'. But the vision is much more solid than that because it is rooted in Christians' experience of God here and now. And a relationship with God cannot end with death; Jesus by his death and resurrection has destroyed the power of death[8].

Some clues regarding the nature of the resurrection life come from the appearances of Jesus after his resurrection[9]. He still bore the marks of nails and spear from his crucifixion, thereby demonstrating that he was the same person. Yet his body was different; it had undergone a substantial transformation. It was not subject to the same limitations; it could appear and disappear at will. Eventually Jesus in his new body entered into heaven—a highly symbolic act, providing a significant window for us into the meaning of resurrection, and known as the ascension[10]

The key word here is transformation. As Paul explained in his letter to the Philippians, 'Our citizenship is in heaven. We await a Saviour from there, the Lord Jesus Christ, who, by the power that enables him to bring everything under his control, will transform our lowly bodies so that they will be like his glorious body[11].' In terms of the dimensional analogy I developed in Chapter 9, the material dimensions will not be absent in resurrection but will be transformed by being linked more strongly with the spiritual dimension.

The vision of the future with which we are presented does not end with our resurrection. New heavens and a new Earth are promised: nothing less than the transformation of the universe[12]. John Polkinghorne points out:

The picture of such a cosmic redemption, in which a resurrected humanity will participate, is both immensely thrilling and deeply mysterious. Yet its unimaginable future has a present anchorage in our hearts ... It is important that the Christian church does not lose its nerve in witnessing to the coherence and divine assurance of such a hope [13].

How the transformation will be achieved is beyond our current ability to imagine, but it is the sure hope of Christians—described and promised by Jesus himself [14]—that in due course, we shall live in the nearer presence of God, where pain, suffering and evil are no more, and where love reigns supreme.

Modern miracles

So far, for miracles of the second kind (those that are scientifically anomalous), I have been considering only those miracles associated with the life of Jesus. We also need to ask whether other miraculous events have occurred or occur today which do not fit into a normal scientific description.

The picture I have presented of God's relation to the universe clearly allows for the possibility of one-off events which, because they are one-off, do not fit the scientific pattern. The arguments are the same as those I put forward in response to the miracles during the life of Jesus: they concern the significance of the events. We may feel, however, that for many events claimed to be miraculous the historical evidence is weak; further, in some cases there may not seem to be a particularly strong spiritual meaning to be conveyed—a miracle must be a 'sign' as well as amazing. For any events, therefore, that are claimed to be in this category, we shall want to look critically at the historical evidence, and to analyze it, so far as that is possible, according to criteria of fitness and consistency from both the scientific and the faith point of view. Inevitably, our limited knowledge and understanding will make it difficult, if not impossible, for us to be categorical about many cases.

Others have considered the evidence for modern miracles much more thoroughly than I can here [15]. I would just like to make three points particularly in regard to our expectation of miracles today.

☐ First, I have constantly emphasized the orderliness of nature and the remarkable consistency of the scientific description, pointing out that these are a reflection of the character of God the creator and sustainer. Christians are aware of God's activity in the usual circumstances of life, which, although entirely consistent with a scientific description, may from the perspective of faith have particular significance which can quite properly be described as miraculous (miracles of the first kind). However, I have already noted that Jesus himself resisted the temptation to interfere with the normal order of nature capriciously[16], and that, apart from miracles of healing, miracles in the sense of events outside the normal scientific order (miracles of the second kind) are surprisingly rare in the New Testament, or, for that matter, in the Bible as a whole.

☐ Secondly, when such miracles are recorded, they often serve a particular purpose of authentication. As we have seen this was particularly the case with those recorded in the Gospels. Again, during the early days of the growth of the church, as recorded in the Acts of the Apostles, miracles of healing were seen as special demonstrations either to support the message being preached or to encourage the new Christian believers[17]. In the subsequent history of the church right up to today, well-substantiated reports of miracles of the second kind are rare. Again, it seems that reports of healing miracles occur more often during particular periods of church growth or when they have accompanied the pioneering advance of Christianity into new areas, for instance, into animist societies, where demonstrations of the power of the Christian God are seen as particularly important[18].

☐ Thirdly, there is the problem of the acquisition of adequate evidence and its interpretation. This can be particularly acute when considering evidence for healing. In many cases where miraculous healing may have occurred, evidence is often not readily available (medical records may be non-existent or incomplete) and different interpretations of the evidence are frequently possible (for instance, spontaneous recovery from some conditions is not unknown). Further, great improvement in physical wellbeing can occur without the removal of all the

183

physical symptoms of disease. Also, as I explained in Chapter 12, healing generally involves much more than physical healing; I emphasized the powerful combination of modern medicine and prayer which is available for the purposes of healing and also noted the possibility of 'spiritual healing' unaccompanied by physical healing[19].

What is vital is that there should be complete honesty in the presentation of evidence for modern miracles. Extravagant claims, backed by inadequate (or sometimes almost non-existent) evidence only serve to bring Christianity into disrepute. This is especially the case where miracles of healing are concerned, because of the danger of giving false expectations to sick people.

God's plan in the world

I want now to return to the nature of God's action in the world. In previous chapters I have frequently referred to God's purposes or God's plan. What can we discern of such a plan? Several objections to the idea of its existence are often put forward. Although I have already referred to some of these in previous chapters, I want to mention them again here and summarize my response to them.

The first objection arises from a common feeling that because so many events are governed by chance, there is no room for a divine plan. This objection has already been addressed in Chapter 6, where I pointed out that chance is not a cause—it does not make things happen. Chance processes can be a valid part of the scientific description but their existence does not invalidate other complementary descriptions, for instance a description in terms of God's action.

A second objection concerns the reality of human freedom. If God has a plan involving us all, does that not make nonsense of human freedom of choice? Yet if, despite all the constraints associated with any given choice, human choices can be freely made, may God's plan not be thwarted?

Here we can recall the arguments of Chapter 7. Our freedom of choice is not illusory, but since we do not yet know where our self-awareness and freedom of action fit in with the scientific scheme of things, we can have little understanding of how God's freedom of action is consistent with our freedom and also with the constraints of order and regularity which we find in the universe.

Various further points concerning this problem have also been made in previous chapters:

☐ First, we are addressing a paradox. Chapter 11 considered two particular paradoxes—one in science, one in theology—which arise because of the limitations of our ability to describe views from different standpoints at the same time. Here is another paradox which arises from a similar confusion—how can God's plan and human free will both operate? We can only expect to have extremely limited understanding of how our view fits in with God's.

☐ Secondly, if God is the creator, then it is he who has brought into being a universe in which creatures called human beings possess the power of freedom of choice— in particular, freedom to respond and freedom to love. In this act of creation God has chosen to limit to some degree his own freedom of action in order to allow his creatures the freedom to respond to him. It is the love of God which draws, not the power of God which coerces.

☐ Thirdly, when God responds to human choices he is not constrained by space and time in the same way that we would be in responding to action by others—a question I have addressed in both Chapters 7 and 12. In particular, our view of God is as creator not only of space but also of time. With this view in mind, we can suppose that God can fit all requirements arising from our choices within his moment-by-moment sustaining activity of keeping the universe going.

I want to suggest two analogies which might help us here. One is of God as a grand master chess player, playing someone of ordinary skill. Both players are acting within the rules of the game. The grand master, however, can be said to have control of the game all the way through, even though his opponent has freedom to make his moves. The skilled master weaves in the moves of his fellow player in order to bring about a victory which is never in doubt, although the character of the end is determined by the moves of both players.

Another analogy, which I introduced in Chapter 4, is that of fault-tolerant hardware, suggesting that God, in his overall design of the universe, has built in a degree of fault tolerance. God's design and plan for the universe can take account of the fact of human freedom. Choices by human beings are real enough, but God, being the great designer that he is, ensures that his purpose is ultimately fulfilled—in particular his purpose concerned with ultimate triumph over evil. I shall have more to say about this in the next section.

No analogies which attempt to parallel God's activity can, of course, be completely satisfactory. The analogies of the grand master chess player and the fault-tolerant designer suggest a God who wants to ensure an end result despite the actions of human beings. That is, however, only part of the story. Although human actions are often negative so far as the purposes of God are concerned, they need not be that way. Rather, they can and should be positive. God invites human cooperation in his work.

Jesus instructed his disciples to be 'the salt of the earth' and 'the light of the world'[20] and to continue the work which he had begun[21]. A further analogy we can use therefore is that we are God's fellow workers[22] or God's stewards[23]. For instance, as God's stewards humans have particular responsibility for stewardship of the Earth and its resources[24].

The moral objection

I have now looked at two of the particular objections to my description of God's action in the world. These have been concerned with the role of chance and the question of freedom. Following on from these, we meet head-on the moral objection. If God is creator, sustainer and controller of all, the greatest conceivable being, what about the problem of evil and suffering? We say that God is good and all-powerful; how can he be both, yet design a universe which includes the possibility of evil and then within that universe allow apparently unrestrained evil and suffering to continue? Why do we not see more miracles in which God clearly restrains evil and rescues people from its worst effects? Where does the reality of evil fit into God's plan?

This is the biggest issue of all to be addressed by religion and, indeed, which we face as human beings. Much has been said and written about it over the years. A number of points are commonly made. For instance:

☐ Much evil and suffering are the result of human sin (sins of neglect as well as of positive harm).

☐ God created people to be free, and the freedom to love implies of necessity the freedom to hate; to be able to choose the good implies the possibility of evil for the choice to have meaning.

☐ Pain provides a necessary signal for us to take care of our bodies.

Such statements may be helpful in facing the problem; they do not, however, provide an explanation[25].

Theologians have tried to come to terms with the issue by defining different categories of 'the will of God'—on the one hand, good events which result from his direct activity, and on the other, evil events which God allows but for which he is not directly responsible. Although it is perhaps helpful to devise terminology which prevents us from directly connecting God with evil, the distinction is bound to appear somewhat contrived. It is interesting to note that the main message of an ancient treatise on the subject, the book of Job in the Old Testament, is the recognition that God is sovereign and that he is in control even of the events associated with Job's suffering. As the book ends, realizing that his view of God has been too small, Job responds, 'I know that you can do all things; no plan of yours can be thwarted.'[26]

Although there seems to be no fundamental explanation (even if one were provided, I suspect that we would not understand it), God has provided a solution. The main problem addressed by the Christian message is the fact of human failure and sin; the heart of the Christian message is that God in Jesus took upon himself the burden of the sin and suffering of the world when he allowed people to nail him to a cross and crucify him. Thus he commends in supreme measure the quality of God's love for human beings and introduces us to a God who is the master of transforming evil into even greater good—a transformation process which is the key to God's overall plan.

As Sir Robert Boyd has written,

If you believe God's choice was unconquerable love, it may not help you to understand why there is pain and evil, but it may do far more to help you accept it than any number of arguments about the existence of good requiring the possibility of evil.[27]

It is not surprising, perhaps, that those who suffer most often turn out to be the greatest saints.

Footnotes

1 John 2:11; 4:54; 6:14; 9:3, 16;11:47, 12:18.

2 See, for instance, Mark 5:43; 7:36, 8.12; Luke 16:31.

3 Mark 2:1–12.

4 Matthew 4:1–10.

5 Matthew 26:53.

6 In Carl F. Henry (ed.), *Horizons of Science*, Harper and Row, 1978, p 16.

7 1 Corinthians 15:35–57.

8 1 Corinthians 15:54–57.

9 Luke 24:13–49; John 20:10—21:23.

10 Luke 24:50–51; Acts 1:9.

11 Philippians 3:20–21.

12 Romans 8:19–22; 1 Corinthians 15:24–28.

13 John Polkinghorne, *Science and Christian Belief*, SPCK, 1994, pp 163–170.

14 John 14:2–3.

15   For instance, M. Poole, *Miracles: Science, the Bible and Experience*, Scripture Union, 1982; *Signs, wonders and healing*, ed. John Goldingay, IVP, 1982; C. Brown, *Miracles and the Critical Mind*, Paternoster Press, Exeter, 1984; *Christian Healing: what can we believe?*, ed. E.C. Lucas, Lynx Books, 1995.

16   Matthew 4:1–10.

17   Acts 3, 5:12–16, 8:7–8, 9:36ff.

18   See for instance Bill Lees, 'Hesitations about Expectancy', in *Signs, wonders and healing*, *loc. cit.*, pp 108–129. That volume presents some useful articles on the debate on modern miracles, especially miracles of healing.

19   *Christian Healing: what can we believe?*, ed. E.C. Lucas, *loc. cit.*

20   Matthew 5:13–14.

21   Matthew 28:19; John17:18; 20:21.

22   2 Corinthians 6:1.

23   Matthew 25:14–30; Luke 12:42–48.

24   See for instance my book *Global Warming: the complete briefing*, Lion Publishing, 1994, Chapter 8.

25   C.S. Lewis, in *The Problem of Pain*, Geoffrey Bles, 1940, provides a helpful discussion of the problem.

26   Job 42:2.

27   In Carl F. Henry (ed.), *Horizons of Science*, Harper and Row, 1978, p 16.

PART 6
Science and Faith

In addressing one of our original questions: if there is a God, what can we learn about him and his connection with us? we have developed a picture of God formed from the complementary descriptions of science (God the great Designer) and faith (God the Person with whom we can be in relationship). But how do these two disciplines reach their conclusions; how do their working methods compare? Chapter 14 examines this problem.

Finally, we need to reexamine the other question with which I began this book: can the hypothesis of God in the spiritual dimension add significance to our material lives? Are science and faith compatible? Chapter 15 considers the extent of the overlap, and outlines the fields of future enquiry where both have significant roles to play in the search for God.

14 Dogma and Doubt

God forceth not a man to believe that which he cannot understand.
JOHN WYCLIFFE

In this chapter I want to describe, from the point of view of the practitioner of science, some of the methods of scientific enquiry and some of the elements which are included, showing that there are similarities to the methods and the elements of religious enquiry[1].

The motto of one of the world's oldest scientific academies, the Royal Society of London, is *Nullius in Verba*. It can be loosely translated, 'Take nothing for granted.' The success of science depends on a thoroughly critical attitude on the part of scientists. Scientific theories need to be given the most rigorous examination. A new theory cannot be accepted until all attempts to falsify it have failed.

In contrast, it is generally assumed that in the realm of faith, much less rigour is required than in science. So much is this thought to be the case that the term 'theology' is commonly used of a body of convictions which is not readily subjected to criticism. If a commentator describes the debate at a political party conference as a theological one, it means that the discussion has become doctrinaire and of little immediate practical relevance. I want to suggest, however, that despite these popular views, there is, in fact, a lot of similarity between the approaches of science and of faith (see also box).

First, let us look in more detail at the scientific approach. A common view of science is that progress is made step by step through relentless logic, each new achievement being based on watertight argument. Attached to each could be the validation Q.E.D.

Although logic and argument have a great deal to do with the scientific enterprise, however, it is not in practice as simple as that. In the first place, we cannot start from scratch; it is essential to build on what has been done already. In fact, a large proportion of the time required to tackle and solve a particular scientific problem will be spent in searching the vast scientific literature for papers of relevance and in extracting from the large body of existing scientific knowledge material which will help in the investigation.

It is common to refer to the body of existing knowledge as the conventional or the accepted wisdom. In this body of knowledge some parts will inevitably be more firmly based than others. But, as with every activity, familiarity with what is known already is an essential prerequisite to further progress.

Critical realism

There has been (and still is) much debate about the relation between a scientific law, theory or model and reality. The philosophy known as critical realism[2] recognizes that the aim of science is to depict reality while also recognizing the fallibility of any given scientific description. It describes well the implicit working philosophy of most scientists, although few articulate their philosophy in a formal way.

The language of science involves much that is in the form of models or metaphors. Science can be confident that its theories, models and metaphors refer to reality, a confidence which is grounded on testing them in practice. However, scientists also recognize that the language, models and metaphors which are employed to describe reality can generally, in the light of new knowledge or data, be improved or revised and are therefore bound to be subject to change[3].

The language of theology in attempting to describe the reality of God is similar to that of science, in that it also employs much in the form of model or metaphor; it is also bound to be very inadequate because there is very little we can expect to understand about God. Compared with the language of science, an important difference is that in theology the central concern is not with impersonal reality but with a personal relationship with God. In order for there to be such a relationship, God has to provide us with a revelation of himself. This has implications for the methods by which we test our descriptions (see Chapter 12).

When it comes to a new scientific idea or theory, an important question is, how does it fit in? Does it accord with observations and experimental facts? Does it fit with our ideas of beauty, elegance and order in nature? Is it economical—in other words, can it describe a wide range of phenomena with the minimum of assumptions?

Take, for instance, the theory of relativity introduced by Albert Einstein in 1905, to which I referred in Chapter 8. Only two assumptions were needed: that the laws of physics are the same within all frames (sets of axes), even though the frames may be moving relative to each other, and that the velocity of light is independent of the velocity of the source of the light. As we saw in Chapter 8, following from those simple but rather fundamental assumptions came predictions concerning the increase of mass with velocity and the equivalence of mass and energy. Elegance and economy were strong features of the new theory, and this readily persuaded many physicists, at the time, of its correctness.

But there were others who were unconvinced. Where, they said, was the experimental proof? A completely unassailable channel of logical deduction could not be provided, and supporting experimental facts were scanty. It was not in fact until 1919 when, during a solar eclipse, it was demonstrated that light rays which pass near the sun are 'bent' (Fig. 14.1) (one of the predictions of the theory), that much of the suspicion was removed. After that, Einstein still had to wait until 1922 for a Nobel Prize; even then it was primarily for his work on the photoelectric effect rather than for his theory of relativity.

It is now relatively easy to accelerate atomic particles to speeds near to that of light and to carry out measurements

FIG. 14.1 Observation in 1919, during a solar eclipse, of the bending of light rays from a star as they passed near the sun, provided an important confirmation of Einstein's theory of relativity. The deviation of the light ray is much exaggerated in the diagram—it amounts to only about one second of an arc (1/3600 of a degree).

SUN

on them, so providing many demonstrations of the accuracy of the predictions of relativity theory. Nevertheless, a typical physics student, if asked to prove the truth of relativity, would be unlikely to quote a particular example, at least until pressed. A more likely argument would be that relativity is so fundamental, and influences so many parts of physics, that it is inconceivable that physics could exist without it.

Relativity is one of those fundamental theories of science whose great strength is that they have brought together ideas and observations from different parts of the subject and integrated them into new frameworks. The work of Clerk Maxwell is another classic example of the power of the integration of ideas. In 1864, he wrote down for the first time the equations which united light, electricity and magnetism into one theory. Thus the foundations were laid for applications in the electric power and communication industries upon which so much of modern life depends.

It should not be imagined that these far-reaching theories of electromagnetism and relativity came completely out of the blue, unrelated to the knowledge which existed at the time. On the contrary, they built on many years, if not centuries, of previous work, of careful experiment and interpretation of experiments carried out by other scientists. Maxwell owed a great deal to the experiments and thought of Faraday. Einstein built on the work of many; Michelson and Morley, Fizeau, Lorentz and Fitzgerald are just some of the well-known names which can be mentioned.

Supposing, therefore, I say that I understand a theory such as the theory of relativity, what do I mean? In the light of the points I have made regarding the scientific approach, three elements can be delineated.

☐ First, I mean that I am familiar with the theory. I have read a lot of books about it, I have answered examination questions on it, I have immersed myself in what it is about.

☐ Secondly, it means that I know how to apply it. Given a physical situation concerning atomic particles, a nuclear power station or light signals in the cosmos, I can work out the result required.

☐ Thirdly, it means that I can see where the theory fits in with other parts of physics. This fitting in may not be complete. In fact, there are bound to be areas of difficulty, uncertainty or seeming contradiction. To that extent my understanding is bound to be limited. But for it to be called 'understanding' at all, it is necessary for these three elements—familiarity, knowing how to apply it, and seeing where it fits in—to be present.

Science has developed by combining an acceptance and appraisal of the existing body of knowledge with a thoroughgoing, critical, questioning attitude. Pieces of the jigsaw are already given; new pieces are continually being added and need to be put into place. Many groupings of pieces, all fitting together well, have already been established. Other groupings fit together less convincingly. New arrangements have to be tried; awkward pieces can be particularly helpful in providing clues as to possible new arrangements. Progress is made by applying an appropriate mixture of dogma and doubt.

Turning now to the theological scene, trying to make sense of the theological jigsaw is not, I believe, very dissimilar from making sense of the scientific one. The same elements which we have already mentioned are involved; namely, becoming familiar with past efforts, interpreting and applying observation and experiment, and integrating ideas.

The basic data of the Christian faith have already been mentioned in Chapter 10. I described there the two 'books': the book of nature, and the person of Jesus, the Word of God. An account of the life and ministry of Jesus, interpreted by his first disciples, is recorded in the Gospels, the Acts of the Apostles and the letters of the New Testament. We also have the history and culture of the Jewish people described in the Old Testament, which provides a necessary background to the events of the New Testament. Then there is the continual record of Christian experience over the centuries, especially perhaps the testimony of individuals we know today[4]. We need to become familiar with all that.

What, then, about the second component of understanding, namely the application of Christian faith? Can I solve problems with it? Here we need to remember that faith is concerned with a personal relationship, not just with a set of facts. Not only my mind is involved, therefore, but all of my being. This personal factor in no way reduces the need for integrity, honesty and critical appraisal. It does mean, however, that the methods of application and the criteria by which the results are judged are bound to be more personal. Commitment is also necessary; not just the intellectual commitment present in the pursuit of scientific enterprise, but the commitment appropriate to the development of personal relationships.

The unique feature of the Christian faith is that the commitment which is required is to Jesus, who is God in human form. It is as I commit myself to the person of Jesus, accepting that he can deal with my problems of guilt and moral failure, that my need for forgiveness and renewal is satisfied.

Although this commitment can be said to be in the spiritual dimension, it is, of course, lived out within the ordinary dimensions of time and space. It is in the world of these ordinary dimensions that my choices are made and my failures occur. It is also in this world where my faith, if it means anything at all, is to be worked out in practice. Jesus, through his life and actions, showed how this can be done. It is not by accident that Christians have often been the initiators in the provision of hospitals and orphanages, prison reform, famine relief and many other caring organizations and institutions; they have followed Jesus' command to love both God and one's neighbour[5].

The third component of understanding I have mentioned concerns the integration of ideas, or seeing things fit together. This is a particularly important component as far as religious faith is concerned, because religious thought must of necessity bring together strands from all aspects of our being and experience, weaving them together into a coherent whole. Knowledge of God, the greatest conceivable Being, Creator and supreme Person, must provide us with a grand perspective from which we can see how the variety of all our experience fits together.

Scientists find it difficult to escape from the conviction, described earlier in the chapter, that some of the basic theories of physical science which enable large parts of the scientific jigsaw to be fitted together, are basically correct. Similarly with the Christian faith, many have found that the fitting together of the two revelations—of God as creator and sustainer on the one hand, and God revealed in Jesus on the other—is so convincing in their experience that they cannot escape the conviction that their faith is basically true. Not that all is seen clearly; even more than in science, faith sees 'but a poor reflection as in a mirror'[6]; but enough of the pattern can be distinguished to provide not only conviction for the mind but a foundation for the whole of life.

The view that the methods of science and religion produce not only different but competing views of the world and of experience is a common one. But it does not stand up to analysis. Belief in a creator within whose creation is centred all our experience—scientific and religious—implies that truth must be seen as a whole. Centuries ago, the apostle John wrote: 'God is light; in him there is no darkness at all.'[7] Much more recently, Albert Einstein remarked, 'Subtle is the Lord, but malicious he is not.' Einstein's life's work was to expound some of God's subtlety found in creation. Christian experience also finds plenty of subtlety in God—the subtlety of light and not the malice of darkness.

Footnotes

1   John Polkinghorne, *Reason and Reality*, SPCK, 1991, expounds this theme much more thoroughly.

2   For an exposition of critical realism in both science and theology, see A.R. Peacocke, *Theology for a scientific age*, SCM Press, 1993, pp 11ff.

3   A.R. Peacocke, *loc. cit.*, p 14.

4   See, for instance, *Real science, real faith*, ed. R Berry, Monarch, 1991.

5   Matthew 22:37–39.

6   1 Corinthians 13:12. Note that mirrors two thousand years ago provided poor images compared with those of today.

7   1 John 1:5

15 Spiritual and Material: Do They Belong Together?

I came to know God experimentally.
GEORGE FOX

If the methods of science and of faith in the search for God are not incompatible, what of their roots? Do they indeed come from the same source? Can we consider the spiritual and the material in one breath?

How do we do science?

Over the past three hundred years science has been extraordinarily successful. Certain factors in the approach to scientific enquiry have been essential to this success; complete honesty and integrity are two particularly important ingredients. In Chapter 14 I described the thoroughgoing critical attitude which is at the basis of science. Facts cannot be preferentially selected to prove a theory. The awkward fact cannot be dismissed; it must be exposed. The belief that truth is out there to be discovered implies commitment to the search for truth, whatever may be the result.

The activity of science is one in which scientists themselves are deeply and personally involved. The scientific process does not just consist of the clinically objective logical steps that are often portrayed (see Chapter 14). As Michael Polanyi has pointed out[1], scientific knowledge, in common with other forms of knowledge, cannot entirely be divorced from the participation and commitment of the scientist. In a rather different but fundamental way our understanding of quantum mechanics emphasizes the importance of the observer. In a quantum-mechanical description an observation cannot be divorced from the presence and the action of the observer—until the box has been opened and viewed, Schrödinger's cat (see Chapter 7) is both dead and alive!

Further, science is not an individual activity but a corporate one. Most scientific work is pursued by groups of people working together. Not only does that mode of working bring together a range of expertise not found in any one individual, it also enables ideas to be discussed and thought through in a cooperative context. The results of one group's work need to be repeated by others and the ideas and theories of that group discussed and tested elsewhere before they can be accepted generally. The progress of science is hammered out in the international scientific arena. Scientists are continually communicating with each other, by letter, by fax, by phone, by electronic mail and by meeting together. Science is perhaps the most cooperative of human activities.

I can illustrate the degree of cooperation from my own experience in the science of climate change, which is currently an area of large public and political concern. During the last few years, I have been privileged to chair and then to co-chair the international scientific assessment for the Intergovernmental Panel on Climate Change (IPCC). In producing our assessments it has been important not just to employ the best expertise so as to deliver the most accurate and comprehensive reports, but also to involve as many scientists from as many countries as possible so that the widest possible consensus could be represented.

We produced our first report in 1990[2], our second in 1992[3] and our third in 1994[4]. Nearly five hundred scientists from over fifty countries assisted with these reports. All of us realized the serious nature of our task and our responsibility to inform policymakers and the public. They needed to know what we were able to say about the likely pattern of future climate change, also what we were certain of and where there was large uncertainty. Despite the uncertainties of the science and its multidisciplinary character, and despite the difficulty of providing useful predictions, a very large measure of consensus was achieved. The final texts of the reports were agreed in meetings of about a hundred scientists representing many countries. Although we argued long, in all three cases there was no dissention in the groups from the final texts we approved. These reports represent one of the largest co-operative scientific assessments ever undertaken and they have been widely acclaimed. It has been a really exciting experience to see a very diverse international group of scientists moving towards agreement not only about the state of scientific knowledge regarding climate change but also regarding the best way to present it to the world.

Why do we do science?

Science appears at first sight to be a very material activity. It is concerned with the material universe, things that we can touch and handle and see. The material benefits science has brought to our lives are commonplace—our work and our leisure are dominated by aids and devices which have been developed as a result of our growing scientific knowledge. The car, the computer, the television, to mention but three, continuously demand our attention. Early this century, Thomas Emerson commented, 'Things are in the saddle and riding mankind.' If it was true then, it is even more true today.

No one has described this takeover by 'things' more eloquently than Theodore Roszak[5], who writes of science with its reductionist approach 'undoing the mysteries', destroying imagination and creating a desert of the human spirit. What he calls the modern technocracy is, he claims, succeeding by its emphasis on the 'systems approach' in its 'coca-colization' of the world. Imagination, he argues, has been replaced by cold calculation in the over-objective emphasis of science.

But if we imagine that the main purpose of science is to provide the base for technological advance, we have missed the most fundamental point of scientific enquiry. The potential usefulness of science was far from the minds of the early experimental scientists. What was driving them was curiosity. They wanted to know about the structure of the universe and how things worked. They exploited the powerful new tools at their disposal, the microscope and the telescope, both opening up exciting new areas for observation. In particular they wanted to know how God had organized the universe and how he ran it. It is these same characteristics of curiosity and wanting to know that have driven scientists ever since.

As we saw in Chapter 2, some scientists go further, especially those who are working in fundamental areas of science such as cosmology and elementary particle physics, and say that they are searching for meaning. Stephen Hawking is looking for 'why it is that we and the universe exist'[6]. Paul Davies invites the readers of his latest book 'to share this scientific excursion into the unknown, in search of the ultimate basis of reality'[7].

The spiritual connections of science

I do not wish to engage in a polemical discussion on the precise meaning of the word spiritual. It is employed in a variety of contexts and expresses a wide variety of ideas. It has to do with things that are not material—with purpose and meaning, with aesthetic values like beauty and elegance, with moral values like goodness and truth and with relationships outside ourselves, for instance with the universe or with other human beings. All sorts of experiences involving elements of these kinds are described as spiritual experiences. For believers in God it has first and foremost to do with our relationship to God—a relationship which overarches all other relationships and which bears on questions of purpose, meaning and value.

With a broad definition of 'spiritual' there are many aspects of the method of the pursuit of science and in the basic attitude of scientists which fall into the spiritual category. The aesthetic content of scientific theories, the requirement for honesty and integrity in the search for truth and the importance of human relationships in the pursuit of science as a cooperative human activity, and supremely the search for purpose and meaning, all possess their spiritual components.

An important element in the attitude of scientists is the idea of transcendence, the idea that in science we are dealing with something objective and 'given'. It is basic to scientific enquiry that there is objective reality to be discovered and described—there is something to be found out 'out there'. The facts and the descriptions resulting from scientific enquiries are not invented by scientists as they pursue their work; rather, they are there to be discovered.

This belief in objective reality is not just associated with the material objects 'out there'. It is just as apparent when concerned with the ideas and the laws which form the basis of the scientific structure of things. As Paul Davies has commented: 'The laws of nature are real objective truths about the universe and we discover them rather than invent them.'[8] But all known fundamental laws are mathematical in form. Are these mathematical descriptions purely human mental constructions, or are mathematicians really uncovering truths that are already 'there'? Roger Penrose argues strongly that mathematicians are discovering objective truth. 'There is something absolute and God-given about mathematical truth,'[9] he writes. 'Not only is the universe "out there" but mathematical truth has its own mysterious independence and timelessness.'[10]

It is key to the idea of the spiritual that we are dealing with something or someone other than ourselves. For some, the realization that the universe is something 'given' engenders an attitude of dependence. Thomas Huxley, a leading biologist of the nineteenth century, commented that 'humility before the facts' is fundamental to scientific enquiry—a comment which echoes words of Francis Bacon, 'The entry into the kingdom of man, founded on the sciences, is not very different from the entry into the kingdom of heaven, whereinto none may enter save as a little child.'[11] After all, we are a part of the universe and dependent upon it for our existence—we saw in Chapter 3 just how much we are dependent on the totality of the universe.

Given that feeling of dependence on the universe for our material existence, it is not difficult to extend that attitude to one of dependence on the One who created and maintains the universe, not just for our material existence but also for the spiritual in our lives. I would argue, therefore, that the religious experience of dependence on God is one which flows naturally from—or, at least, is consistent with—the basic presuppositions of science.

Not everyone, however, wants to feel dependent on God. After all, we human beings stand apart from the rest of the universe; we can observe the universe, we can understand it—at least to a substantial degree—and we can use it. So why not ourselves try to be in control—to be God? That is the most fundamental temptation we all face.

Adam and Eve in the Genesis story[12] gave way to that temptation as they plucked the fruit from the tree of knowledge of good and evil which had particularly been forbidden. By doing so, they were attempting to take for themselves what can only be given. Many human beings (indeed, all of us at one time or another) still act in the same way, and nowhere is this more clear than in the unrelenting pursuit of power and control through technology. Rather than acknowledge our dependence on God as creator of the universe, humans attempt to set themselves up as the transcendent beings from whom all else flows.

New Age ideas and science

A number of different strands are included in the 'umbrella' body of ideas and practices known as New Age philosophy, some with their roots in eastern religions. Parallels have been drawn between some of the insights of quantum mechanics, which emphasize unity and interconnectedness in physics, with religious ideas[13]—for instance, those that emphasize the strong interactions which exist between humans, their environment and the rest of creation. However, despite the attempts to marry ideas from fundamental physics with New Age ideas, much of New Age philosophy is opposed to the presuppositions of science[14]—this is perhaps not surprising, as a driving force of the New Age movement has been the anti-science and anti-technology attitudes of recent decades.

One of the differences between the thinking of New Agers and the basis of scientific enquiry is that they question the objective nature of reality; for them there is no ultimate reality and no ultimate truth. For them truth is subjective rather than objective, a matter of feelings as much as, if not more than, reasoning.

Such an attitude is encouraged by an overemphasis on the power of technology which fails to recognize the very different attitudes latent in the science on which technology is based: the search for truth, purpose and meaning; the attitude of 'humility before the facts'; the need for value judgments as well as the drive for progress. If scientists and non-scientists alike were made more familiar with the basic stuff of scientific thought and the ingredients which have led to important scientific discoveries, the temptation to use technology to play God might be less strong.

A quite different approach is taken by what is often called New Age philosophy (see box). The New Agers lay particular stress on the oneness of the universe. One of their aims is to feel comfortable in the universe and not alienated from it—an alienation common in our technology-dominated society. Two comments from well-known scientists illustrate this feeling of remoteness and alienation: Stephen Weinberg's remark, 'The more the universe seems comprehensible the more it also seems pointless,'[15] and the words of Jacques Monod, 'The ancient covenant is in pieces; man at last knows that he is alone in the unfeeling immensity of the universe out of which he emerged only by chance.'[16]

But we do not have to espouse New Age ideas to feel comfortable in the universe or in harmony with it. We have seen how much we are part of the universe—the whole universe is needed for us to be here. Flowing from this are attitudes of dependence and humility that form the basis of a harmonious relationship between human beings and the universe. The Christian would go further and say that feeling comfortable with the universe connects strongly with feeling comfortable with God.

In the creation story at the beginning of the book of Genesis we find God 'walking in the garden in the cool of the day'[17] in order to converse with Adam and Eve. I wonder what they talked about on those evening walks! The intricacies of creation, I think, could have been one of their themes. As humans, created in the 'image of God'[18], we can understand what it means to be creative. Further, even though part of the universe, we are able to view it transcendentally, somewhat as God does, as something outside ourselves, to enjoy, to control and, so far as we are able, to look after.

The New Biology

I began, in the early chapters, with a description of the physics of the cosmos and have since used illustrations, mostly from physics, to illuminate the interface between scientific and religious thought. I have also referred to the revolutions this century not only in physics, with the discovery of quantum mechanics, but also in biology, with the discovery of the structure of DNA, the birth of molecular biology and the science of genetics. An increasing integration between the natural sciences of biology, chemistry and physics has resulted from these revolutions. The new insights thus generated have led to a recognition that some areas of research, such as behavioural biology or the study of information processes in the brain, need to be viewed in an even wider context and require an even broader integration of scientific fields. I particularly want to mention in this context developments in the biological sciences.

Some of these have been addressed by Arthur Peacocke[19], who describes, for instance, the mechanisms for biological development which have been suggested by the interplay between law and chance in the genetic structure of living systems. He goes on to suggest that a similar interplay provides mechanisms for the development of aspects of human personality and behaviour. In doing this, he reflects on the implications for theology.

The scientific fact that matter ... can in man become self-conscious and personal, self-transcendent and corporately self-reflective is a fundamental feature of the cosmos and must be regarded as a clue to its meaning and intelligibility.[20]

In Chapter 7 I posed the challenge which the existence of human consciousness and free will presents to fundamental physics, and noted that a grand shake-up of our present picture of physical reality may be required. I mentioned also the similar challenge presented to biology if it is adequately going to include these qualities—human consciousness, self-awareness and free will—within its purview[21].

This challenge is not just to traditional biology but more particularly to the fields of psychology, the behavioural sciences and sociobiology (which studies the connections between biology and human behaviour). It is here, in the discussion of the origins of and the influences on human behaviour, that a potential conflict between the scientific and theological points of view arises.

☐ The evolutionary biological process is dominated by the requirement for survival, whether it be of genes, individuals, groups or species, a theme Richard Dawkins has eloquently developed in his book *The Selfish Gene*[22]. Sociobiologists tend to interpret human behaviour in terms of the need to survive. Some seemingly altruistic behaviour can assist in survival, and therefore can be motivated by our basically selfish drive. Even religious belief is credited with survival value. Michael Ruse and Edward Wilson suggest that the possession of a moral code or of moral beliefs is 'an illusion fobbed off on us by our genes to get us to cooperate... ethics is a shared illusion of the human race.'[23]

☐ Most theologians, on the other hand, talk of absolute moral values and of codes of behaviour which appear to run counter to biological survival. The Christian ethic goes beyond loving our genetically close neighbours—it demands that we look after the weak and needy and that we love and do good to our enemies.

Is there a real conflict here? While theologians clearly need to come to terms with and learn from the new insights of biology, biologists for their part need to understand more of the potential capabilities possessed by human beings. We are endowed with the innate capability to learn from experience; in other words we are biologically equipped to supersede our biology[24]. Further, we also need to be sure that we avoid the reductionist trap[25]. The fact that we can describe biological or socio-biological mechanisms which play a large part in the determination of human behaviour does not imply that there are not equally valid and complementary descriptions of another kind. Two lovers would very likely be unimpressed by being told that they were merely being driven by a genetically-based requirement for the survival of the race.

In the letters of Paul found in the New Testament, a contrast is drawn between two driving forces in human nature, 'flesh' and 'spirit'[26]; by 'flesh' Paul meant that in us which is in rebellion against God, a symptom of which is the selfishness linked to our basic biological instincts. By 'spirit' he meant that in us which comes from our relationship with God, and which is dominated by love—love for God and for our fellow human beings. Sin comes from giving in to the desires of the 'flesh'. Paul described the battle which goes on within all of us: 'I have the desire to do what is good but cannot carry it out[27].' The Christian solution which Paul expounds is to bring God into the battle; he emphasizes the importance of a relationship with God, that with the help of God's Holy Spirit the battle can be won[28].

This basic moral dilemma which all of us experience has a strong connection with our biological make-up driven by 'the selfish gene' and the need for survival. As Peacocke comments,

In man it almost appears as if the evolutionary process has faltered, for man's tragedy is both to be aware of his potentialities and to be unable to attain them.[29]

Has science anything to say about such matters? Many scientists believe that it has. Some would argue that religion is outmoded in its ideas and appeal and that science as we know it can provide answers to such questions. Although no particular solutions are offered, they point out that the methods of science, have proved so powerful and effective, it is not unreasonable to suggest that they can also address moral and religious issues. Paul Davies, for instance, claims that science offers a 'surer path than religion in the search for God'[30].

I believe it is entirely proper for science to study such issues; the mistake which is being made by many scientists is that they try to do so while ignoring the resources of faith. A much wider view needs to be taken, a view which is non-reductionist and holistic—which means that the study of human attitudes and behaviour must not be over-dominated by the strictly biological. All relevant areas of knowledge need to be included—psychological, moral, social and religious, including the possibility of a relationship with God. Rather than being an area of possible conflict, this is one where scientists and theologians can effectively work together.

Science and theology working together

At the heart of Christian belief are creation, incarnation and resurrection—that God the creator and sustainer of the universe took upon himself human form in the person of Jesus, and that Jesus died and rose again from the dead with a transformed body. Any theology of the relation between God, humanity and the universe has to be built round these central components of the Christian story. In fact, it has to be built round the person of Jesus because it is Jesus who as God, as the agent of creation[31] and as a human being belongs uniquely to all three—God, humanity and the universe.

These links which exist in the core of Christianity between the material and the spiritual were emphasized by William Temple, Archbishop of Canterbury in the 1930s. He wrote,

It may be safely said that one ground for the hope of Christianity that it may make good its claim to be the true faith lies in the fact that it is the most avowedly materialistic of all the great religions. It affords an expectation that it may be able to control the material, precisely because it does not ignore it or deny it, but roundly asserts alike the reality of matter and its subordination. Its own most central saying is: 'The Word was made flesh' ... By the very nature of its central doctrine Christianity is committed to a belief ... in the reality of matter and its place in the divine scheme.[32]

Because of these strong connections between the spiritual and the material, there are a number of areas where the results of scientific work nudge up against religious belief. Let me summarize some of those I have mentioned here and uncovered in preceding chapters:

☐ Firstly, there is the position of humans in the universe in the light of the insights of cosmology that the universe is extremely finely tuned, and that the whole history of the universe is needed to provide for human emergence.

☐ Humans can understand with their mathematical and physical tools the laws that govern the structure and dynamics of the universe, including their own emergence. They can even search for a 'Theory of Everything'!

☐ Humans can reflect on their own emergence, their position in the universe and search for overall meaning.

☐ Humans possess qualities of consciousness, self-awareness and freedom of thought and action, the scientific understanding of which requires fundamentally new theories and insights.

☐ Humans have moral goals which are not based on the need for survival; they also recognize their inability to meet those goals.

The first three of these are insights which arise from our scientific knowledge and which have strong influence on theological thought. The last two are ones where we can expect theological insight in its turn to influence science. The origins of these particularly human characteristics and their significance is an appropriate study for scientists and theologians to undertake together.

Mystery

Throughout this book, we have been trying to think about God, indeed trying to describe God, putting together parts from our scientific and religious experience. But our attempts to describe what must be indescribable and our attempts to know what must be unknowable are bound to be woefully inadequate. Surrounding it all is something which is an essential component of religious experience (and not unknown in the scientific quest)—the element of mystery.

Science has its illuminated areas of knowledge, its penumbra and the dark areas of shadow not yet investigated. Religion too has its illuminated area of knowledge, its penumbra of unclear reflections and partial shadows. In this analogy it is in the sun itself—the source of illumination—that the mystery of God resides—an image taken up by Paul[33]. Colin Morris has described religion as a counterpoint between knowledge and mystery[34]. He goes on to say:

We talk about creation as revealing God, and natural theology is built on that proposition. But you could equally well argue that the purpose of creation is to hide God, because we could not withstand the intolerable impact of total reality. Demosthenes said, 'If you cannot bear the candle, how will you face the sun?' How could we bear the total impact of the reality of God? Which is why God said to Moses, 'No man can look at my face and live'…..It is this urge to look at the sun which has driven on religious minds from the beginning of time, and they have ransacked human knowledge to find images of this otherness of God (another word for holiness); Plato writing about flickering shadows on the wall of a cave; Isaiah in that beautiful image describing God passing by, and you cannot see him, but you can hear the rustle of his garment; the whisper of God's ways; Paul talking of baffling reflections in a mirror. The magnetism of mystery.'

But this God, surrounded in mystery, is also 'the God that would be known' (to use the title of the recent book by John Templeton and Robert Hermann[35]). To enter into something of the mystery of God we do not have to try to look into the sun of his presence—that would only blind us. Instead, God has revealed himself to us in his creation and in the person of Jesus. Mystery is still there in creation—our scientific advances do not reduce this mystery, but rather enhance it. And Jesus is a further expression of the mystery of God[36]. He uniquely combines the material and the spiritual—both God and human in one person.

In Chapter 11 I presented this as a paradox and suggested that it is not unlike the paradox in physics about the nature of light: does light consist of waves or of particles? The answer is that it is both waves and particles, but in giving that answer we emphasize the limitations of language in setting up an adequate model—a limitation we are only too conscious of in the expression of religious ideas.

In Christianity there is a balance between knowledge and mystery, and maintaining this balance is vital for us. Too much knowledge without mystery and we imagine we are in control. Give us mystery without knowledge and we withdraw from the real world. More knowledge leads to more mystery, both in science and in religion, and a balanced mixture of knowledge and mystery leads us to appropriate humility, and enables us to dig deeper into both.

Practical outworking

Let us now address what this marriage between the material and spiritual means in practical terms; how does it affect the way we think or the way we live? I want to bring together five points which have mainly been covered in earlier chapters.

☐ First, as I expounded in Chapter 13, it affects the way we pray. It is in the context of our personal prayers that the material and the spiritual are brought together for us as individuals, and it is in the context of corporate prayer that they are brought together for the church and for the world.

☐ Secondly, as I pointed out at the end of the last chapter, it affects our view of life after death. Christians believe that the resurrection of Jesus demonstrates that humans have potential for new life after death, in transformed bodies[37]. In the terms of our dimensional analogy, we have the promise that the new spiritual dimension will become much more real—which provides enormous impetus to us to enter more into that dimension now. There are further implications: Jesus' resurrection foreshadows the eventual transformation not just of human beings but of the whole of creation[38].

☐ Thirdly, it influences our attitude to health and healing. The close relation between the material and the spiritual serves to underline one of the messages of Chapter 13, where I emphasised the need to put spiritual ministry alongside medical treatment.

☐ Fourthly, it affects our view of the quality of life. In November 1991 I took part in a discussion organized in Vienna by the International Council of Scientific Unions (ICSU) on the likely needs for science and technology next century. We were a very international and multidisciplinary group of about 200 scientists, including social scientists. One of the 16 'themes' of the conference was the 'quality of life'. Although we could

---

Science and the quality of life

In preparation for the United Nations Conference on Environment and Development—the 'Earth Summit'—held in Rio de Janeiro in June 1992, the International Council of Scientific Unions (ICSU) organized a conference on the likely needs for science and technology next century. The work of the conference was centred around 16 themes: water, energy, technology, capacity building, and so on. Theme 12 was entitled 'quality of life'[39].

Basic human material needs contributing to the quality of life were listed: food; shelter; earnings; health; environment; protection; interpersonal contacts; education and recreation. Also listed were non-material contributing factors: freedom; cultural and religious pursuits; creativity; social encouragement of altruism, generosity, equanimity and solidarity; social discouragement of aggressiveness, savage competition and discrimination. Experts from the scientific disciplines (including the social sciences) represented at the conference identified contributions which they would be able to make towards the enhancement of the quality of human life next century.

largely agree on those factors which ideally make up quality of life (see box), as scientists we could say virtually nothing (and there was considerable debate on the issue) about how to achieve it in practice. In particular how could we overcome the inherent selfishness, greed and other undesirable characteristics shown by human beings? The problems can be described by science, as can the factors which may exacerbate them, but science cannot solve them. That is where the religious dimension comes in. The Christian faith tackles that problem head on and offers a solution.

☐ Fifthly, it provides a strong impetus for us to deal with the worldwide problems which are increasingly being brought to our attention. Western society has many material goals: economic growth, social welfare, better transport, more leisure and so on. But for our fulfilment as human beings we desperately need not just material challenges, but challenges of a moral or spiritual kind. I have referred (see box) to the Earth Summit at Rio which addressed some of the major issues facing us as we look forward to a new century. Paramount amongst these is the threat to the global environment, arising from the rapid growth in human population and in the demand for natural resources.

Science and technology have a large role to play in the solution of the enormous problems we face. But on their own they are inadequate; they can even be harmful. Value judgments are also required, together with an attitude of respect for the natural world and mutual respect for each other as human beings. The appropriate relationship for us to have with the Earth is often described as one of stewardship, which implies that we are carrying out our duty as stewards on behalf of someone else—but of whom? Some would see no need to answer the question specifically, others talk of acting on behalf of future generations or of a generalized humanity. But a religious person would want to be more specific and say that we are acting on behalf of God—we have a God-given responsibility[40] to look after the Earth. Further, in facing the problems involved we are not meant to act independently of God but rather in partnership with him, as indeed the word 'stewardship' implies.

'Seeing'

Throughout this book, I have put a great deal of emphasis on the need for the widest possible scientific view. Physics, so successful at describing events as remote as the earliest moments of the Big Bang, needs to be expanded, if not revolutionized in order to take into account the behaviour of the human brain and the existence of consciousness. Biology, with its fundamental developments of recent years, is becoming more integrated with other sciences. Medical science is realizing the importance of a holistic approach which accepts the strong links between the physical, the mental and the spiritual.

Theology by its very nature should have very wide horizons. God, after all, if he is God at all, is involved in everything. Yet so often our view of God is a limited one; we allow him to be present in the spiritual side of life, but give him little say in more material things.

I have been at pains to point out the two revelations of God—the revelation in nature and the revelation in the person of Jesus. I began by suggesting that including God in the scientific picture is like the inclusion of perspective in a picture. But a picture is still a two-dimensional image. Adding God's self-revelation in Jesus is like having binocular vision of a three-dimensional scene. An appreciation of depth is present when a scene is viewed with both eyes or through a pair of binoculars rather than through one eye. Even more depth can be apparent when a pair of pictures is viewed through a stereoscope. Our appreciation of God is very flat unless we look at the whole range of his activity in an integrated way.

This analogy of 'seeing' is often used in talking of scientific understanding. After having worked on a particular problem for years, sometimes a scientist just 'sees' its solution; a momentary experience and all can seem to fall into place. I have already referred in Chapter 7 to

Roger Penrose's view of the importance of 'seeing' in mathematics. He writes:

We must 'see' the truth of a mathematical argument to be convinced of its validity. This 'seeing' is the very essence of consciousness ... When mathematicians communicate, this is made possible by each one having a direct route to truth, the consciousness of each being in a position to perceive mathematical truths directly, through this process of "seeing". [41]

In Chapter 13 I mentioned examples, cited by Penrose, of unusual inspiration which have been experienced by some eminent mathematicians as ideas or solutions have come to them 'in a flash'. I mentioned, too, that artists or musicians have similar experiences: Mozart could see an entire and complicated composition as a whole before he began to write it down. At a much more mundane level many of us have experiences when suddenly we exclaim, 'Oh, I see!'

Religion claims to be the most integrating subject of all. Since it is concerned with our relationship to the greatest Being of all, that is bound to be the case. It is not surprising therefore that 'seeing' is a term that is often used about religious belief. Contrary to the popular phrase, faith is not blind; it is something we acquire when we 'see'; we talk for instance of the eye of faith. Sometimes this insight comes in a flash, as with Paul on the Damascus road [42]; sometimes it develops much more slowly. As with scientific 'seeing', after the first sight, faith needs to be tested in a whole variety of ways.

Science and faith are not poles apart. Both are searching for reality and truth. Their methods possess many similarities and their areas of concern overlap—they are bound to do so, as the human searchers are the same in each case. Our thinking in both can be stretched and our understanding deepened by widening their purview and by putting them together. As we delve deeper into both areas of knowledge we realize even more their excitement and their challenge, and how very much more there is to discover.

The final paradox

I began by talking about the search for meaning and the search for God. A common experience of those who pursue this search is the discovery that God is quietly but intently searching for them. If you feel that God is pursuing you, don't play hard to get!

Footnotes

1   M. Polanyi, *Personal Knowledge*, University of Chicago Press, 1958.

2   *Climate Change: the IPCC Scientific Assessment*, J.T. Houghton, G.J. Jenkins, J.J. Ephraums (eds), CUP, 1990.

3   *Climate Change 1992. The Supplementary Report to the IPCC Scientific Assessment*, J.T. Houghton, B.A. Callander and S.K. Varney (eds), CUP, 1992.

4   *Climate change 1994*, ed. J. Houghton *et al.*, CUP, 1995.

5   In *The making of a counter-culture*, Faber and Faber, 1968 and *Where the wastelands end*, Doubleday, 1972.

6   S. Hawking, *A brief history of time*, Bantam Press, 1988, p 175.

7   Paul Davies, *The mind of God*, Simon and Schuster, 1992, p 22.

8   Paul Davies, *op. cit.*, p 84.

9   R. Penrose, *The Emperor's New Mind*, OUP, 1989, p 146.

10   Martin Gardner in the foreword to Roger Penrose's book *loc. cit.*

11   Quoted by D.M. Mackay, *The open mind*, *loc. cit.*, p 86.

12   Genesis 3

13   See, for instance, F. Capra, *The Tao of Physics*, Harper Collins, Flamingo, 1976.

14   For a critique of New Age thinking see Ernest Lucas, 'Scientific Truth and New Age Thinking', *Science and Christian Belief*, 4, 1992, pp 13–25.

15   S. Weinberg, *The first three minutes*, Andre Deutsch, 1977, p 154.

16   J. Monod, *Chance and Necessity*, Collins, 1972, p 167.

17   Genesis 3:8.

18   Genesis 1:26.

19   A.R. Peacocke, *God and the New Biology*, J.M. Dent, 1986.

20   A.R. Peacocke, *loc. cit.*, p 129.

21   G. Edelman, *Bright air, brilliant fire; on the matter of the mind*, Penguin Books, 1992.

22   R Dawkins, *The Selfish Gene*, OUP, 1976.

23   M. Ruse and E.O. Wilson, 'The evolution of ethics', *New Scientist*, October 17, 1985, pp 50–52, quoted by Peacocke, *loc. cit.*, p 113.

24   David Booth, personal communication.

25   A.R. Peacocke, *loc. cit.*, devotes several chapters to problems of reductionism in biology.

26   Romans 7:18, 8:4ff, Ephesians 2:3. The word translated 'flesh' in the Authorized Version of the Bible is translated 'sinful nature' in the New International Version.

27   Romans 7:18.

28   Romans 8:5.

29   A.R. Peacocke, *loc. cit.*, p 130.

30   P. Davies, *God and the New Physics*, J.M. Dent, 1983, p 229.

31   John 1:3

32   W. Temple, *Nature, Man and God*, Macmillan, 1964, 1st ed. 1934, p 478, quoted by Peacocke WHERE.

33   1 Timothy 6:16

34   In a sermon reported in *Mission and Complexity*, pp 148–56, The Christ and the Cosmos Initiative of the Methodist Church, 1991.

35   Harper and Row, 1989.

36   Revelation 10:7.

37   Luke 24, John 20, 21.

38   Romans 8:20–21. See also C.A. Russell, *The Earth, Humanity and God*, UCL Press, 1994, Chapter 10.

39   *An Agenda of Science for Environment and Development into the 21st Century*, ed. J.C.I. Dooge *et al.*, CUP, 1992, Chapter 12, 'Quality of life', pp 227–238.

40   See for instance Genesis 1:28.

41   Roger Penrose, *loc. cit.*, pp 541, 554.

42   Acts 9:1–9.

Glossary

Anthropic Principle (the) Scientific theory that the whole formation and development of the universe has been necessary in order for humanity to develop.

Atom The smallest unit of an *element* that can take part in a chemical reaction. Composed of a nucleus which contains *protons* and *neutrons* and is surrounded by *electrons*.

Bifurcation A critical situation for a variable quantity in any system when either of two choices can be made with minimal energy expenditure, hence where either choice is equally likely.

Big Bang (the) Scientific theory of how the universe was formed by rapid expansion from a concentrated initial state of extremely high density and temperature.

'Brain-story' The description of physical, chemical and biological processes in the brain. See also *'I-story'*.

Chaos A mathematical theory describing systems which are extremely sensitive to small perturbations; small discrepancies in the initial conditions will lead to completely different outcomes when the system has been in operation for a while. For example, the motion of a pendulum when its point of suspension undergoes forced oscillation will form a particular pattern as it swings. Started from a slightly different position, it can form a completely different pattern, which could not have been predicted from studying the first one.

Complementarity The validity of different descriptions of the same events considered from different points of view.

CQG theory A theory posited by the physicist Roger Penrose called Correct Quantum Gravity, which would revolutionize our way of thinking about physics.

Consciousness Self-awareness. A quality possessed by human beings. The extent to which it may be possessed by higher animals is a matter of debate.

Dualism The idea that mind and body are two separate entities.

Electron Negatively charged component of the *atom*.

Element Any substance that cannot be separated by chemical means into two or more simpler substances.

Entropy The tendency towards increasing disorder in the universe expressed by the second law of thermodynamics.

Faith In its religious connotation, a system of belief. In this book it denotes a relationship of trust with a personal God, including both reasons for belief and motivation for action.

'Faith story' The description of events which looks for God's action in the world. See also *'scientific story'*.

Fault tolerance Fault-tolerant equipment is designed so that if it is faulty or damaged it can still function.

Flesh A term used by the apostle Paul to denote the part of human nature in rebellion against God.

God of the gaps The concept of God which looks for divine activity only in those areas which are not yet understood, hence which dwindles as scientific knowledge increases.

Gödel's theorem The mathematical proof descovered by Kurt Gödel that whichever mathematical system is chosen, some true facts will be unprovable using the given system.

Heisenberg Uncertainty Principle The principle that either the momentum or the position of an electron can be established with accuracy, but not both.

'I-story' The conscious experiences and choices experienced subjectively by each human being. See also *'brain-story'*.

Imaginary quantities Quantities employed in mathematics which involve the square root of -1, designated by the letter i. Minkowski *space-time geometry* involves imaginary time.

Immanence God's presence within space and time. See also *transcendence*.

Incarnation The process of God becoming a human being.

Induction A method of mathematical proof in which the desired result is assumed, and then tested against known data.

IPCC Intergovernmental Panel on Climate Change—the United Nations body assessing global warming.

Jesus First-century Jew believed by Christians to be divine as well as human. See also *incarnation*.

Miracle An unusual event having spiritual significance (such as a sign of God's presence) which may (but need not) involve a suspension of the currently-understood laws of science. See also *resurrection*.

Molecular biology The study of biology at the level of *molecules* interacting with each other. It is particularly concerned with molecules such as DNA which self-replicate and carry genetic information.

Molecule Two or more *atoms* of one or more *elements* chemically combined in fixed proportions.

Neutron A component of most atomic nuclei without electric charge, of approximately the same mass as the *proton*.

New Age A group of ideas and philosophies with roots in eastern religions which, in general, promotes attitudes that are pro-environmental but anti-technology and anti-science.

Newtonian mechanics Mechanics based on the classical laws and equations formulated by Isaac Newton which, it was thought, provided entirely deterministic and predictable descriptions of the physical world.

No-boundary condition Mathematical concept developed by the physicist Stephen Hawking which implies that the universe had no beginning.

Non-linear equations Mathematical equations in which one variable plotted on a graph against another does not give rise to a straight line.

Nuclear fusion (synthesis) The process whereby two nuclei at the correct energy levels for *resonance* fuse and release energy; it gives rise to the energy radiated by the sun. See also *relativity*.

Photon A particle of light.

Prayer Communication with God; an expression of a relationship with God.

Proton A positively charged component of the atomic nucleus.

Quantum mechanics A system of mechanics developed by physicists during the twentieth century to describe the behaviour of very small (subatomic and atomic) particles. See also *Schrödinger's cat*.

Reductionism The philosophy that the behaviour of the whole can be understood by the summing of the behaviour of the parts.

Relativity Theory introduced by Albert Einstein which asserts that all motion is relative, that no velocity can exceed the velocity of light in a vacuum, and which leads to an expression of the equivalence of mass and energy.

Resonance The condition needed for two atomic nuclei to bond together, depending on each nucleus having the right level of energy.

Resurrection *Jesus'* rising to life after being killed by crucifixion. Christians also believe in resurrection after death, involving both physical and spiritual characteristics.

Schrödinger's cat A thought experiment set up by the physicist Erwin Schrödinger, in which a cat inside a sealed box is either killed or left alive. Until an observer looks inside the box and discovers the outcome, by *quantum mechanical* rules the cat is deemed to be both dead and alive.

'Scientific story' The description of events according to scientific theory. See also *'faith story'*.

Sin Rebellion against God.

Space-time geometry A geometry invented by the mathematician Minkowski, in which time and space are equally treated as dimensions. It is consonant with Einstein's theory of *relativity*.

Spiritual dimension An analogy or model to assist in thinking about God's presence outside the universe is to consider that in addition to the three dimensions of space and one of time, there is a fifth dimension—the spiritual dimension—in which God is to be found.

Stewardship The attitude that human beings should see the Earth as a garden to be cultivated rather than a treasury to be raided.

Thermodynamics The study of heat as a form of energy. See also *entropy*.

Transcendence God's presence out of space and time. See also *immanence*.

Trinity (the) A model of God developed in the first few centuries AD in which God is described as a unity but involving three persons (Father, Son and Holy Spirit).

Two Books (the) An idea developed during the sixteenth-century reformation in the Western church that God could be found in two books: the book of nature and the person of *Jesus*.

Wave-particle duality Light displays properties both of a wave and of a particle, depending on the experiment chosen; thus demonstrating the incompleteness of either description.

Index